Exploring the Evidence for Creation

Henry Morris III

HARVEST HOUSE PUBLISHERS
EUGENE, OREGON

Scripture quotations are from the King James Version of the Bible.

Cover by Dugan Design Group, Bloomington, Minnesota

Cover photo © Anton Balazh / Fotolia

EXPLORING THE EVIDENCE FOR CREATION
Copyright © 2008/2009 by Institute for Creation Research
Published by Harvest House Publishers
Eugene, Oregon 97402
www.harvesthousepublishers.com

Library of Congress Cataloging-in-Publication Data
   Morris, Henry M.
   Exploring the evidence for creation / Henry M. Morris III.
      p. cm.
   Originally published: Dallas : Institute for Creation Research, © 2009.

   ISBN 978-0-7369-4721-3 (pbk.)
   ISBN 978-0-7369-4722-0 (eBook)

   1. Evolution. 2. Creationism. 3. Creation. 4. Bible and evolution. I. Title.
   BL263.M583 2012
   231.7'652—dc23

                        2011048729

Printed in the United States of America

12 13 14 15 16 17 18 19 20 / VP-SK / 10 9 8 7 6 5 4 3 2 1

Acknowledgments

This book is a distillation of nearly four decades of scientific research conducted by the dedicated men and women of the Institute for Creation Research.

My father, Dr. Henry M. Morris, the founder of ICR, wrote more than 60 books, many more booklets and pamphlets, and literally hundreds of articles during his 36 years on the job. Much of what has been written about creation science in the last half century is due in large part to his intellect, training, and passion for the proper understanding and articulation of God's truth, particularly related to Genesis.

Early on he was joined by Dr. Duane Gish, who became a renowned debater on college and university campuses, fiercely defending the accuracy of the biblical model for the origin of life as well as exposing the emptiness of the evolutionary claim of transitional fossils in the geologic record.

Other researchers joined the science faculty as word of our work spread. Dr. Steve Austin, considered one of the most knowledgeable creation geologists in the world today, became active as a field geologist for ICR and began his three-decade research at the Grand Canyon, followed by nearly a decade of active field work on Mount Saint Helens.

Ken Ham was on the ICR team for several years before he left with our blessing to establish Answers in Genesis and the Creation Museum in Petersburg, Kentucky.

Senior research scientist Dr. Larry Vardiman coordinated the groundbreaking project on isotope dating called Radioisotopes and the Age of the Earth (RATE). This eight-year study involved all of the scientific staff at ICR along with several others with whom ICR had established adjunct relationships.

For the past ten years, my brother Dr. John Morris has served as president of ICR. A geologic engineer and former professor, John has written a number of popular books dealing with the core issues in the creation–evolution debate.

Many others who have worked at ICR or are working here now have written articles or books for us, and their materials have been adapted for use in this book.

A number of years ago, Richard Pferdner, director of Internet ministries for ICR, told me of his vision to broaden the reach of ICR through an easy-to-use collection of many of the evidences found in the following pages. That vision has been a great motivation to complete this book.

The labor of writing has been complemented by the editorial oversight of Lawrence Ford, director of communications for ICR, and his superb staff, with special thanks for the careful review by Beth Mull and Brian Thomas, who have been instrumental in making sure that the material is readable and accurate.

Gene Skinner and the rest of the staff at Harvest House Publishers have been such an encouragement as they have taken this material and transformed it into the fine work you hold in your hands today.

Rare is the book that is written without any help or encouragement. So it is with this work. I am grateful to all who have been involved and trust that the truths in this book will impact the lives of many and cause us all to extol the wonders of our Creator.

Henry M. Morris III, DMin
Chief Executive Officer, Institute for Creation Research
Dallas, Texas

Contents

Preface

Why Read This Book?

In the beginning, God created…"
Does the God described in the Bible really exist? Is it plausible to believe that an omnipotent, omniscient being has existed eternally? And did that God really create everything in the universe? Or did everything that exists develop over billions of years as a result of the random interaction of stellar gas?

It is man's nature to question life and the world around him. Who am I? How am I different from the other creatures on earth? Am I just a higher order of animal, a freak accident of nature's infinite cycle of accidents over billions of years? Could I possibly be created in the image of God, or am I merely the fittest of animals, now able to use everything within my power for my own pleasure? Is my sole purpose in life to fulfill those personal desires—to simply survive—or was I, a member of humanity, designed to serve and glorify something or Someone much greater? Is life an exquisite work of art or a cosmic joke at man's expense?

There are two very different views on these fundamental questions. These views, or worldviews or belief systems, hold their own presuppositions that we use every day to interpret the meaning of everything around us. Some have suggested that all presuppositions can be summarized by two types of information filters: atheist, which presupposes that God does not and cannot exist, and creationist, which presupposes that God is the originator and sustainer of everything.

Obviously, these two are diametrically opposed to each other.

Those who presuppose that God does not exist look at everything from a purely naturalistic viewpoint. Everything is to be explained without God in the story. Those who presuppose that God does exist attempt to understand everything in light of what that God has revealed, both in His creation and in the information that He caused to be recorded through human authors over the millennia.

This book rests firmly on a creationist worldview.

If the creationist worldview is true, we should expect to discover real, tangible, and observable evidence that supports its fundamental tenets. The God of Scripture invites our investigation: "Prove me now herewith, saith the LORD of hosts." Indeed, if God does exist, there ought to be plenty of evidence that He exists. If there is no God who designed the cosmos, that should also be clear.

This book presents evidence to validate the creationist worldview.

We tend to look for answers from the limited experience and knowledge of our own lives, but the answers we seek are freely given by the One who created us. God's very existence is witnessed in the creation, and His immutable truth is clearly proclaimed for all to observe. Even science itself—we might even say, especially science—verifies the hand of a Creator in our universe. The Bible, unique and beautiful in its account of human history from the beginning, becomes the foundational textbook in which we begin our search for truth.

> God's very existence is witnessed in the creation, and His immutable truth is clearly proclaimed for all to observe.

The Bible describes the first humans, Adam and Eve, as nothing less than the personal "hands-on" creations of God, endowed with His unique image. You and I, the direct descendants of that first pair, bear that same image. If this is so, and man was truly designed by God, then he is loved deeply by Him as well.

The universe, including the earth and all life and especially mankind, were created by God. The message of Scripture is undeniable. And as a result of what God has revealed about Himself and what He made, every question that man could ask about life, purpose, and himself is answered in the Bible.

But evidence for God's existence and His special creation also abounds beyond the sacred text of Christianity. His existence, His truth, and His work are all clearly seen through science, reason, and nature. God's love for His creation compelled Him to clearly communicate how important it is that all people know how they were formed and what meaning their lives are to have on earth. As important as the truth of God's creation and His love for man is, why wouldn't He provide evidence from so many realms?

Part 1 of this book details the evidence for God and His creation in these five categories:

> Evidence for God
>
> Evidence for Truth
>
> Evidence from Nature
>
> Evidence from Science
>
> Evidence from Scripture

Part 2 of this book briefly explains the five primary reasons why recent creation is accurate both biblically and scientifically.

> The Bible does not allow an evolutionary explanation.
>
> Science does not observe evolution happening today.
>
> There is no evidence evolution took place in the past.
>
> God's character absolutely forbids evolutionary methods.
>
> God's purpose for creation precludes evolution.

May God richly bless you as you explore the evidence for creation!

Part 1

Exploring the Evidence for Creation and the Creator

1

Evidence for God

The fool hath said in his heart, There is no God.
Psalm 14:1

*There is still something that is unexplained...the basic
laws of nature...Who created these laws? There is no
question but that a God will always be needed.*
Barry Parker

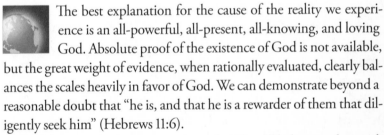 The best explanation for the cause of the reality we experience is an all-powerful, all-present, all-knowing, and loving God. Absolute proof of the existence of God is not available, but the great weight of evidence, when rationally evaluated, clearly balances the scales heavily in favor of God. We can demonstrate beyond a reasonable doubt that "he is, and that he is a rewarder of them that diligently seek him" (Hebrews 11:6).

God has promised numerous times that He will help us understand what He has done for us. Indeed, His promises ensure our discovery of His existence—if we really want to know the truth.

> I know the thoughts that I think toward you, saith the
> LORD, thoughts of peace, and not of evil, to give you an
> expected end. Then shall ye call upon me, and ye shall go
> and pray unto me, and I will hearken unto you. And ye
> shall seek me, and find me, when ye shall search for me
> with all your heart (Jeremiah 29:11-13).

If that promise is true, we ought to be able to "see" God in the physical world in such a way that knowledge of God would be obvious or intuitive through our everyday experience. And in fact, that is exactly what God promises. "The invisible things of him from the creation of the world are clearly seen, being understood by the things that are made, even his eternal power and Godhead" (Romans 1:20). Even the "invisible things" are "clearly seen" in what is available to all of us. Are you aware that all of science rests on an invisible law?

Cause and Effect

The most certain and universal of all scientific principles is that of causality, or the law of cause and effect. The implications of this principle have been fought over vigorously in theological and philosophical disciplines, but there is no question of its universal acceptance in the world of experimental science and in ordinary experience.

During the first century AD, Saul of Tarsus became so convinced that God was real that he changed his name to Paul and spent the rest of his life as a Christian activist. In fact, he became so famous that on his trip to Athens, the intellectual elite of that sophisticated city invited him to speak to the philosophical leaders at the renowned amphitheater on Mars Hill (next to the Acropolis). During his discourse, Paul told these men that they were looking for spiritual satisfaction in all the wrong places. The evidence for God was all around them—even in their own humanity. "Forasmuch then as we are the offspring of God, we ought not to think that the Godhead is like unto gold, or silver, or stone, graven by art and man's device" (Acts 17:29).

Scientific interpretation: We are here, so the cause for humanity must be greater than us but similar to us. Since the dawn of time, it has been observed that people only come from people.

Everything has a cause.

In ordinary experience, one knows intuitively that nothing happens in isolation. Every event can be traced to one or more events that preceded it and in fact caused it. We ask casually, "How did this happen?" or "What caused this?" or "Where did this come from?" Sometimes we try to get at the beginning cause (or first cause) by asking, "When did it start?" or more incisively, "Why did this happen?"

When we try to trace an event to its cause, or causes, we find that we never seem to reach a stopping point. The cause of the event was itself caused by a prior cause, which was affected by a previous cause, and so on.

Police investigators at an accident scene, for instance, use the principles of cause and effect to determine who was ultimately responsible for the accident and how it happened.

Eventually, we must face the question of the original cause—an uncaused First Cause.

A scientific experiment is a test that relates effects to causes in the form of quantitative equations, if possible. Thus, if one repeats the same experiment with exactly the same factors, he should get exactly the same results. The very basis of the scientific method is this very law of causality—that effects are in and like their causes and that like causes produce like effects. Science in the modern sense would be altogether impossible if cause and effect should cease. This law inevitably leads to a choice between two alternatives: (1) an infinite chain of nonprimary causes (nothing is ultimately responsible for all observable causes and effects), or (2) an uncaused primary Cause of all causes (the one absolute Cause that initiated everything).

Effects point to a cause.

Rationally, we can conclude that all things began with a single uncaused First Cause: the God who is above all and existed before all other causes.

The first universal law demonstrates the existence of an uncaused source, or a First Cause, by which observable effects came about. But we also see two more related universal laws demonstrated in everything we examine in the world around us. No new mass/energy (that is, matter) is generated anywhere in the universe, and every bit of the original mass/energy is still here. Every time something happens (that is, an event takes place), some of that energy becomes unavailable.

The first law of thermodynamics tells us that matter can be changed but cannot be created or destroyed. The second law tells us that all phenomena (mass/energy organized into an effect) continually proceed to lower levels of usefulness. In simple terms, every cause must be at least as great as the effect that it produces and will actually produce an effect that is less than the cause. That is, any effect must have a greater cause.

When we trace this universal law backward, we are faced again with the possibility of an ongoing chain of ever-decreasing effects resulting from an infinite chain of nonprimary, ever-increasing causes. However, what appears more probable is the existence of an uncaused and ultimate Source—an omnipotent, omniscient, eternal, and primary First Cause.

What are the logical implications?

These principles of cause and effect indicate that the Cause for the universe in which we live must be an infinite First Cause of all things. Random motion or primeval particles cannot produce intelligent thought, nor can inert molecules generate spiritual worship.

The First Cause of limitless space must be infinite.
The First Cause of endless time must be eternal.
The First Cause of boundless energy must be omnipotent.
The First Cause of universal interrelationships must be omnipresent.
The First Cause of infinite complexity must be omniscient.
The First Cause of spiritual values must be spiritual.
The First Cause of human responsibility must be volitional.
The First Cause of human integrity must be truthful.
The First Cause of human love must be loving.
The First Cause of life must be living.

We would conclude from the law of cause and effect that this First Cause of all things must be an infinite, eternal, omnipotent, omnipresent, omniscient, spiritual, volitional, truthful, loving, living Being!

God's Omniscience

Contrast these two quotes about God's omniscience.

> The *omniscient* God knows all that can be known given the

sort of world he created…In our view God decided to create beings with indeterministic freedom which implies that God chose to create a universe in which the future is not entirely knowable, even for God.[1]

I am God, and there is none like me, declaring the end from the beginning, and from ancient times the things that are not yet done, saying, My counsel shall stand, and I will do all my pleasure (Isaiah 46:9-10).

One of the recent debates among evangelical theologians is the extent to which God knows things. The contrast between the two statements above is sufficient to expose the difference. The verses above insist that that the omniscient God knows everything (including the future), though some would suggest that the omniscient God knows only that which exists (which allegedly does not include the future).

God's omniscience is observable.

Several passages point to a body of evidence that is "clearly seen" in the created universe. Psalm 19:1-4 and Romans 1:18-25, the classic examples, speak of "knowledge" and "speech" that demonstrate God's eternal power and divine nature. The text of God's Word has much to say about the infinite mind of the Creator. In Christ are hidden "all the treasures of wisdom and knowledge" (Colossians 2:3).

The infinitely complex nature of this universe has become more observable over the past few decades. From the vast majesty of the stellar host to the microscopic beauty of living things, we are becoming more and more aware of the incredible design, order, and interrelated purposes of our world. Indeed, the intelligent design movement gains its momentum from these very facts.

God's omniscience requires functional perfection.

Everything revealed about God, both in the universe and in the Scriptures, shouts the message that God is a God of order, purpose, and will, with no hint of randomness. God does not react to circumstances. He is never forced to change His mind about His reason for doing something. He does not alter His plan for eternity, nor does He get confused about His design, His pleasure, or His purpose.

> The counsel of the LORD standeth for ever, the thoughts of his heart to all generations (Psalm 33:11).

> [God has] made known unto us the mystery of his will, according to his good pleasure which he hath purposed in himself...We have obtained an inheritance, being predestinated according to the purpose of him who worketh all things after the counsel of his own will (Ephesians 1:9,11).

God's omniscience must produce perfect purpose and order.

God's omniscience demands that God create absolutely and only the best—whether at the scale of the universe or of the molecule. He could not and would not experiment. He knows, so He must do. He could not and would not produce an inferior product. He must create, shape, and make only that which is good.

God's omniscience is in absolute conflict with evolutionary mechanisms.

Evolution from simple to complex life over vast ages requires both experimentation with creation and the creation of inferior forms. In evolution, there is no permanent good. Atheistic evolutionary scholars have long understood that the philosophy of evolutionary naturalism requires the use of processes and the sanction of activities that are the opposite of God's nature.

> The evolutionary process is rife with happenstance, contingency, incredible waste, death, pain and horror...[The God of theistic evolution] is not a loving God who cares about his productions...[He] is careless, wasteful, indifferent, almost diabolical. He is certainly not the sort of God to whom anyone would be inclined to pray.[2]

Perhaps the more sad commentary is that only Christian scholars compromise their position on the creation of the world. The evolutionists and atheists do not.

The Triune Universe

There is an immeasurably and unimaginably huge universe out there (even though the most important part of it appears to be here). The physical universe is temporal—its physical characteristics are defined qualitatively and quantitatively in and by space, time, and mass/energy (matter).

Any effort to determine the cause of the universe is purely hypothetical. No human was there to observe the processes, so any attempt to understand events of prehistory (especially original events) must therefore be based on a belief system rooted in certain presuppositions. The theories and ideas may be many, but the presuppositions can only be of two sorts: (1) There is an infinite series of causes, going back into infinite time, with no ultimate Cause, or (2) there exists an uncaused First Cause that was external or transcendent to the universe.

Describing the nature of the universe by means of a finite mind and very limited life experience is a bit subjective to say the least. Apart from information that would have been observed at the time by an intelligent being, the interpretation of the data that we can now glean from our various telescopes or microscopes (as sophisticated as we may believe they are) is really nothing more than complex speculation.

The universe contains speech and knowledge from the hand of the Creator Himself. Mankind would do well to read His "book."

God entered time, space, and matter.

Many scientists today conduct their research based on their presupposition or belief that nothing exists beyond the natural world—that which can be observed around us—and thus they do not accept that any ultimate Cause exists.

Scientists at ICR hold to the presupposition that the uncaused First Cause is the Creator who exists outside of the physical creation He made. Time is not eternal, but created. To ask what happened in time before time was created is to create a meaningless false paradox. There was no "before" prior to the creation of the triune universe of time, space, and matter.

Yet even more amazing (and the universe *is* amazing) is the historic fact that this Creator-God, after purposefully creating the space-time-matter universe, chose to enter it in the God-man, Jesus Christ, for the sole purpose of providing the means by which humanity could have a personal relationship with the Creator. "The Word was made flesh, and dwelt among us, (and we beheld his glory, the glory as of the only begotten of the Father,) full of grace and truth" (John 1:14).

Time, space, and matter point to the triune Godhead.

> For this cause I bow my knees unto the Father of our Lord Jesus Christ, of whom the whole family in heaven and earth is named, that he would grant you, according to the riches of his glory, to be strengthened with might by his Spirit in the inner man; that Christ may dwell in your hearts by faith; that ye, being rooted and grounded in love, may be able to comprehend with all saints what is the breadth, and length, and depth, and height; and to know the love of Christ, which passeth knowledge, that ye might be filled with all the fulness of God (Ephesians 3:14-19).

This text encapsulates the doctrine of the Trinity in the Bible. This truth, taught in many other passages of the New Testament, is undoubtedly the most distinctive doctrine of the Christian faith. Most religions are either pantheistic (this includes some forms of Buddhism) or polytheistic (as is Hinduism). Two other religions are monotheistic (Judaism and Islam), but only Christianity recognizes the Triune God—Father, Son, Holy Spirit—one God in three persons.

The sacred book of the Muslims—the Koran—regards Jesus as only a prophet, repeatedly denouncing as infidels all those who believe in the Trinity. The Jews often consider Jesus to have been a great teacher but no more than that. To the Christian, however, the Lord Jesus Christ is a person and yet God incarnate, God's only begotten Son, the Creator, Savior, King of kings and Lord of lords. Christians also believe that the Holy Spirit is not just a spiritual influence, but a real person, the third person of the Godhead.

God is the infinite, invisible, omnipresent Father of all. But He is also the Son, who is visible and touchable and yet the perfectly holy Word who is always revealing and manifesting the Father. And God is also the Holy Spirit, always present to guide, convict, and comfort. A majestic mystery, but a wonderful reality! Three divine persons, each equally and totally God.

We cannot adequately comprehend this reality with our finite minds, but we are compelled to acknowledge it and believe it and rejoice in our hearts. And this reality of God's triune nature is somewhat analogous to space in God's created universe. Space is comprised of three dimensions, each of which permeates all space. This structure is helpful to illustrate the nature of the triune God. He is one God, not three gods, yet He is revealed as three persons, each of whom is eternally and completely God.

The apostle Peter also noted the action of every person of the divine Godhead in the great work of saving those who trust in Christ: "[To the] elect according to the foreknowledge of God the Father, through sanctification of the Spirit, unto obedience and sprinkling of the blood of Jesus Christ: Grace unto you" (1 Peter 1:2).

It seems that God Himself has made such a model. "The invisible things of him from the creation of the world are clearly seen, being understood by the things that are made, even his eternal power and Godhead" (Romans 1:20). That is, the creation itself can be seen as a model of the three-in-one Godhead.

> The creation itself can be seen as a model of the three-in-one Godhead.

Space, both invisible and at the same time the matrix in which all of our reality exists, is analogous to the heavenly Father. "No man hath seen God at any time" (1 John 4:12). But "in him we live, and move, and have our being" (Acts 17:28).

Matter is the visible and tangible revelation of the existence of space. We see space by means of the visible phenomena present in it. Just so, God the Son is the Word (John 1:14) that makes it possible for us to see God. "He that hath seen me hath seen the Father" (John 14:9). In Jesus Christ "dwelleth all the fullness of the Godhead bodily" (Colossians 2:9).

Time is the means by which we experience our reality. Matter is really mass/energy operating in a very specific way through time. Were there no time, nothing would function—nothing would happen. And that "event fulfillment" is the ministry of the Holy Spirit. He is the One who causes us to be "born again" (1 Corinthians 6:11). He is the One who imparts the spiritual gifts of God to the believers (1 Corinthians 12:8). Indeed, the Holy Spirit is the One who guides into truth (John 16:13) and brings conviction about the need for truth (John 16:8).

The only accurate illustration of the triune God is given by the Creator Himself by the "things that are made."

The physical universe is, in a very real sense, a trinity of trinities. Also, in a certain sense, human life is a trinity of body, soul, and spirit. In fact, tri-unity in various ways is often seen in the creation. (However, note that a trinity is not an entity composed of three individual parts, like the sides of a triangle, but rather an entity of three parts, each of which is the whole.)

Although no man could ever model the Godhead, God has seemingly done this in His creation. The third mention of the Godhead is in Colossians 2:9: "For in [Christ] dwelleth all the fullness of the Godhead bodily." Thus, the Lord Jesus can say to His disciples, "He that hath seen me hath seen the Father" (John 14:9), for He Himself is "the image of the invisible God" (Colossians 1:15).

Design and Purpose

Human beings are unique from every other living organism in the world, specially created and specially purposed. The earth is also like no other planet, specially created by God for humans, and we can easily observe evidence of His design in His creation.

Beauty

Aesthetics is the study of beauty, usually associated with art. However, the discipline itself and the philosophical apologetics related to the concept extend into every sphere of imagination, sensibility, and taste. God saw that His creation was good, in appearance as well as in all other sensory aspects, and humans can behold beauty only because He first caused beauty to exist.

Essentially, the foundational argument suggests that because the concept of beauty exists (even if it is in the eye of the beholder), there is an ultimate standard by which beauty is judged. Determining the aesthetic value of anything requires rational judgment, even though that judgment is unique to each individual. Each rational judgment must rely on one's ability to discriminate at a sensory or emotional level.

This examination makes a judgment regarding whether something is beautiful, sublime, disgusting, fun, cute, silly, entertaining, pretentious, discordant, harmonious, boring, humorous, or tragic. And, of course, since such ability exists only in the mental acuity of imaginative appreciation, the Source of such ability must also be both rational and emotional.

The vast differences between individual tastes and even between cultures, both in time and in location, speak to the enormity of such possibilities and to the unfathomable wonder of the hunger for beauty in every human being.

That such a hunger exists only in human beings is a wonder in itself! The flower is not impressed with its own majesty; it merely exists with no conscious awareness. The chimpanzee does not gaze longingly on the enigma of the *Mona Lisa,* nor do the stars muse on the heavens they themselves grace.

The chimpanzee does not gaze longingly on the enigma of the *Mona Lisa,* nor do the stars muse on the heavens they themselves grace.

In fact, all humanity eschews destruction and random chaos as ugly and attempts to mask death with various levels of cosmetic disguises. Clearly, some sights and sounds are not beautiful, so there must exist a standard of perfect beauty.

AESTHETICS HAS NO PLACE IN DARWINISM

Darwinism teaches that all creatures evolved by slowly morphing from a single first living thing. Varying environments were imagined by Charles Darwin to press new features into creatures over eons of time. Thus, all features should trace their origins to a survival need, as different environments forced creatures to invent new survival features. However, many animals have features with no apparent survival-related function. Instead, they just look good.

Darwin himself was vexed, for example, over the brilliance of peacock feather colors. They do not serve any vital function, like legs or teeth or a heart, so Darwin imagined that they had evolved by female birds' mate preference for showy feathers. However, recent research has shown no such correlation between mate matching and peacock plumage. Peacock feathers could simply be adornments that display God's creativity. Psalm 104:24 says, "O Lord, how manifold are thy works! in wisdom hast thou made them all: the earth is full of thy riches."

Animal play is similar. Even after decades of searching among all kinds of mammals, birds, and even reptiles and insects, Darwinists have been unable to link play with survival. Theories abound, but data so far do not support any of them. In one experiment, monkeys were raised in total isolation from other individuals and from any objects of play. Once released, the creatures survived just as well as the control group. The poor monkeys simply missed out on some fun!

One giant marine reptile was apparently created for the purpose of having fun. "There go the ships: there is that leviathan, whom thou hast made to play therein," says Psalm 104:26. Darwinism has failed to explain beauty and play, but both have their place in the context of creation.

Justice

Our postmodern age has redefined right and wrong in terms of subjective feelings and personal perspectives. Yet despite the passing of the ages, humans still have an innate sense of absolute right and wrong. Why? Because God Himself is just.

Morality involves the study of the universal recognition that good is better than evil, which logically requires the existence of an ultimate Judge. That is, since all humanity accepts the knowledge that certain events and standards are better than others, even though cultures may differ on what those events or standards may be, there must be an ultimate Source of such thinking, even if the absolute standard has become distorted over time.

C.S. Lewis, one of the most prolific writers and thinkers of our time, wrote of what he called Moral Law, or the Law of Human Nature, in his work *Mere Christianity.*

> The Moral Law, or Law of Human Nature, is not simply a fact about human behaviour in the same way as the Law of Gravitation is, or may be, simply a fact about how heavy objects behave. On the other hand, it is not a mere fancy, for we cannot get rid of the idea, and most of the things we say and think about men would be reduced to nonsense if we did. And it is not simply a statement about how we should like men to behave for our own convenience; for the behaviour we call bad or unfair is not exactly the same as the behaviour we find inconvenient, and may even be the opposite. Consequently, the Rule of Right and Wrong, or Law of Human Nature, or whatever you call it, must somehow or other be a real thing—a thing that is really there, not made up by ourselves.[3]

We find then that we do not exist on our own, that we are under a law, and that Somebody or Something wants us to behave in a certain way.

Therefore, this Somebody or Something is directing the universe, and as a result we sense an internal law that urges us to do right and makes us feel responsible and even uncomfortable when we do wrong. We have to assume this entity is more like a mind than it is like anything else we know, because after all, the only other thing we know is matter, and you can hardly imagine a bit of matter giving instructions.

Catholic apologist and philosophy professor Peter Kreeft writes, "The only possible source of absolute authority is an absolute perfect will."[4]

Love

We cannot scientifically prove the existence of love, just as we cannot prove the existence of gravity and aerodynamics. Yet we know love exists and can observe its effects. Animals can display affection, but only humans are capable of receiving, giving, refusing, and rejecting love.

Animals (including chimps) are not able to provide any assistance to other creatures they are not related to, and they even seem to be unable to recognize the needs of other animals. Although some animals (especially such mammals as dogs, cats, and horses) appreciate affection, only humans are capable of love.

Humans are driven by an entirely different kind of love. We love our children when they are disobedient. We can love our enemies and sacrifice our lives for our friends (as soldiers do). The highest, truest kind of love is that which consciously seeks and takes practical action to do good for someone else, valuing that other person higher than one's self, even if providing such good requires self-sacrifice. This is what separates human love from the affection expressed by animals.

Of course, if God did not create us, how would we ever know what real love is, much less learn to practice love ourselves? The very fact that we can love and be loved (by God and by others) is yet another proof of a Creator's love. Because of His own nature of infinite love and grace, God was pleased to create beings on whom He could bestow His love and grace and who, being made in His image, would be capable of reciprocating and responding to that love. "God commendeth his love toward us, in that, while we were yet sinners, Christ died for us" (Romans 5:8).

Meaning

Humans in particular seek a reason to exist and for the most part have difficulty believing that we are simply here to consume the earth's resources and die. God created the heavens, the earth, and all living creatures—especially mankind—with special purposes in mind, which He explained in His Word. Every part of creation has a specific meaning and purpose for existing, which we can most easily observe in the study of various ecosystems.

In contrast, here is the essence of the naturalistic-evolutionary story.

There is no God (or god is in the forces of nature or in man himself). Nothing supernatural exists (except perhaps some extraterrestrial race of superintellects that have evolved in other parts of the universe). No evidence exists for the God of the Bible, so we can be certain that there is no such thing as a plan for your life. Thus, there is no afterlife. Speculative Hollywood movies notwithstanding, and the many reported out-of-body experiences to the contrary, no rational naturalist believes in any form of eternal life. When you're dead, you're dead!

Such hopeless beliefs drive many into lives of debauchery and hedonism, and fill the couches of psychologists and psychiatrists all over the world. Teenage suicide is alarmingly high, and therapists themselves continue to manifest one of the highest suicide rates in civilized countries. Scandals abound among the leaders of world business, politics, and churches. "If in this life only we have hope in Christ, we are of all men most miserable" (1 Corinthians 15:19).

There is no good news in evolutionary theory.

There is, however, glorious wonder and life-changing power in the "everlasting gospel" (Revelation 14:6), which includes...

- power to transform (Romans 12:2)
- power to enrich (2 Corinthians 9:11)
- power to bring satisfying peace to all situations (Hebrews 13:20-21)
- power to change the mortal body into the immortal and everlasting being that will live eternally with the Creator (1 Corinthians 15:53-54)

Conventional wisdom says, "Grab all the gusto you can; you

only go around once in life!" We are told, "Just be yourself," and "Let the good times roll." These and hundreds of other clichés sprinkled throughout our culture misdirect our thinking and undermine real satisfaction, purpose, and meaning in life.

God designed humanity to enjoy the happiness of stability, productivity, and success (see Psalm 1). Jesus said, "I am come that they might have life, and that they might have it more abundantly" (John 10:10).

Ideas Have Consequences

"Argument weak at this point. Thump podium and holler louder!"

This joke is quoted derisively from time to time to demonstrate that arguments are based on presuppositions that are logically and empirically weak. *Every* idea, religion (belief system), and scientific theory has foundational concepts that cannot be proved by physical means and intellectual acumen.

This is so commonly understood and widely accepted that we rarely think about this ubiquitous condition. Everybody believes in something. Even the atheist believes that there is no God, but there is certainly no way to prove such a concept. All men and women have faith that their particular presuppositions provide an adequate basis for their actions and lifestyles. That broad set of presuppositions is also known as a worldview.

Dallas Willard relates a concept in his book *Divine Conspiracy* that he occasionally shares in his classes.

> In our culture one is considered educated if one "knows the right answers." That is, if one knows which answers are the correct ones. I sometimes joke with my students at the university where I teach by asking them if they believe what they wrote on their tests. They always laugh. They know belief is not required. Belief only controls life.[5]

Belief controls life. Now that piece of wisdom is important! Jesus said it this way:

> A good man out of the good treasure of his heart bringeth
> forth that which is good; and an evil man out of the evil
> treasure of his heart bringeth forth that which is evil: for of
> the abundance of the heart his mouth speaketh (Luke 6:45).

Belief controls life. Ideas have consequences.

What you believe determines what you think.

What you think dictates what you do.

And what you do dominates your life.

In 1981, Francis Schaeffer wrote *A Christian Manifesto* as a response to the 1973 *Humanist Manifesto II*. He opened his critique of the humanist's thinking by noting that many Christians uncritically accept an incorrect worldview.

> The basic problem of the Christians in this country in the
> last eighty years or so, in regard to society and in regard
> to government, is that…they have failed to see that all
> of [society's problems have] come about due to a shift in
> world view—that is, a fundamental change in the overall
> way people think and view the world and life as a whole.
> This shift has been *away from* a world view that was at least
> vaguely Christian in people's memory (even if they were
> not individually Christian) *toward* something completely
> different—toward a world view based upon the idea that
> the final reality is impersonal matter or energy shaped into
> its present form by impersonal chance.[6]

This wholesale shift in thinking has so permeated the evangelical church that many Christians struggle with the concept of an almighty, omniscient Creator to whom they must answer one day. The pervasive symptom of this change in thinking is the shift away from trusting the revealed Word of God as an absolute source of truth from the God who cannot lie (Titus 1:2).

According to many evangelical churches, the Bible may contain truth, but no one can be certain of its authority, accuracy, or applicability. Science has supposedly rendered the early chapters of Genesis either useless as history or downright deceptive. Scholars have uncovered so-called new secrets about the Lord Jesus and about the Bible. Famous preachers, politicians, and celebrities loudly proclaim allegiance to Jesus, only to be exposed in some scandal that would embarrass the heathen.

We have come far—but certainly not in the right direction! Can we correct our course?

> Wherewithal shall a young man cleanse his way? by taking heed thereto according to thy word. With my whole heart have I sought thee: O let me not wander from thy commandments. Thy word have I hid in mine heart, that I might not sin against thee (Psalm 119:9-11).

May the heart of the great Creator, whose word spoke the heavens into existence, draw us this day into a certainty about His inspired Word of truth.

Order

Ordered systems or structures do not happen spontaneously. We never observe orderliness occurring by accident—that is, without an intelligent cause to direct the order. No amount of undirected power or energy is enough to bring order out of chaos. Try shooting a wristwatch with a bullet; the order of the components does not increase! (The only order in a watch is that which the watchmaker intelligently puts into it at the beginning.)

> We never observe orderliness occurring by accident—
> that is, without an intelligent cause to direct the order.

Likewise, if we drop a plain glass bottle of spoiled milk onto bricks, it quite naturally shatters into a more disorderly arrangement: chaotic glass fragments mixed with spilled spoiled milk. It could never reform itself into a more exquisitely sculpted glass container containing fresh milk!

The addition of huge amounts of energy is not enough either. A tired human eats to gain food energy, but eating hot coals is not an adequate energy source because it fails to match and cooperate with the orderly design of human digestive systems.

Everyday experiences, such as breaking watches and spilling milk, remind us that order does not happen by itself. In fact, our entire universe demonstrates that same truth. The earth's rotation, the moon cycle, and the changing seasons are just a few of the ordered processes observable in nature. These processes don't happen randomly—God causes them.

God is the Author and Organizer of orderliness. His design and construction of our own bodies, through the complexity of biogenesis, is a good reason to glorify and thank Him for making us. As wild and untamed as our world is, everything in nature follows a specific order orchestrated by God.

Wisdom

All organisms react to their environments, but human beings are the only creatures capable of rationalizing and acquiring knowledge and wisdom. That is because only humans are made in the Creator's image.

Wisdom is essentially the effective understanding and use of information. Humans discover information; we do not invent it. Through wisdom (that is, by using information effectively), humanity has developed a set of scientific laws that elegantly express reality in the language of mathematics. Johann Kepler, the noted founder of physical astronomy, is said to have considered his science to be "thinking God's thoughts after Him."

The unfathomable intelligence that invented the universe and preprogrammed its interactive workings displayed a wisdom beyond imagination. In particular, the cause of our universe coming into being, and of its continuing to operate as it does, is a dynamic display of the Creator's wisdom, some of which we can scientifically understand and effectively apply. When we do, we are "thinking God's thoughts after Him."

> The cause of our universe coming into being,
> and of its continuing to operate as it does, is a
> dynamic display of the Creator's wisdom.

The very fact humans have any wisdom at all, not to mention the wisdom necessary to understand a meaningful amount of the workings of the universe, is more amazing than the marvelous physics of the universe itself! How can an immaterial mind, residing inside a human body made mostly of water (along with other elements of the earth), comprehend anything—even this sentence?

Only by God's creative grace can human beings think any thoughts at all and especially thoughts that are logical and analytical enough to be called scientific.

Summarizing the Evidence

Cause and effect. A cause must be greater than its effect, so the First Cause of time and love must be eternal and loving.

The triune universe. The dimensions of time, space, and matter reflect the triune nature of the Spirit, Father, and Son.

Design and purpose. Without God, order and meaning would not exist. Neither would right and wrong.

Biblical Insight

In Acts, Paul twice addressed pagans who had little or no knowledge of the Scriptures. Compare Acts 14:15-17 with Acts 17:22-32.

1. How did Paul begin each address?

2. How did Paul introduce each particular audience to the Creator? Why was it prudent for him to use this approach?

3. How can Paul's pattern be applied or misapplied today?

Evidence for Truth

*Buy the truth, and sell it not; also wisdom, and
instruction, and understanding.*

Proverbs 23:23

*The truth is incontrovertible. Malice may attack it,
ignorance may deride it, but in the end, there it is.*

Winston Churchill

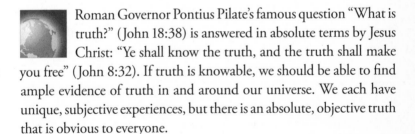 Roman Governor Pontius Pilate's famous question "What is truth?" (John 18:38) is answered in absolute terms by Jesus Christ: "Ye shall know the truth, and the truth shall make you free" (John 8:32). If truth is knowable, we should be able to find ample evidence of truth in and around our universe. We each have unique, subjective experiences, but there is an absolute, objective truth that is obvious to everyone.

Natural Laws

Inescapable laws in nature exist for our benefit, our advantage, and our protection. We can observe these laws in action all around us.

Science is founded on absolute truth.

Scientific knowledge requires an absolute standard of truth that can be discovered. Scientific knowledge is not a collection of subjective opinions. Rather, it is a collection of explanations about objective reality based on observed or predicted phenomena. These explanations must be verified repeatedly to confirm that they correctly model reality.

As our technical ability to observe reality improves, we are able to increase the quality and quantity of our observations. Better-observed data challenge our explanations, some of which will no longer fit the observed facts. New theories are then formed and either verified or falsified.

Our scientific knowledge changes rapidly, but the absolute reality being modeled has never changed. The scientific method assumes an absolute reality against which theories can be verified.

> The scientific method assumes an absolute reality
> against which theories can be verified.

Empirical science is based on observation.

The scientific method compares our limited understanding with the absolute truth of reality. It requires the scientist to test a theory based on observed or predicted facts. The scientist must formulate a theory or hypothesis based on what has been observed and then design a test by which the theory may be verified as valid or not.

If the theory produces observed events that correspond with the theory postulated in advance, the scientist has a serious beginning point from which to claim further science (knowledge) about the specific test.

During the past several hundred years, a number of theories have been repeated so often that they are now considered scientific laws. Scientists are confident that these laws correctly model the absolute truth of reality. Should someone claim to have had a subjective experience that contradicts one of these laws, the burden of proof is on that person to prove that he can repeatedly demonstrate that the law is false. The standard of measure remains absolute truth about reality, verified through repeated observation.

WHY TRUTH IS UNDENIABLY TRUE

Something must necessarily be true. This can be assuredly known by examining truth claims that attempt to deny truth. For example, some say, "There is no truth." But is this claim true? If so, it refutes itself. Thus, it cannot possibly be true.

Self-refuting claims are nonsense. They violate the law of non-contradiction. This law observes that "no two contradictory statements can both be true at the same time and in the same sense."[1] *A* is not non-*A*. This, along with a whole suite of similar laws, constitutes the core mental machinery required to think and speak and communicate with God and one another.

"There is no reality, only perception," is another self-refuting claim. Can the idea that there is no reality actually be real? If there is no reality, then the truth claim itself is not real!

Interestingly, the opposite of self-refuting claims are undeniably true. For example, it is not possible to deny the truth claim "Truth exists" without using a truth claim in the very attempt to deny it.

Some things are undeniably true, so it is possible that the Bible is true. All that remains for the inquirer is to investigate the Scriptures and find out. Evidences related to the Bible are explored in chapter 7.

Historical science requires assumptions.

Scientists observe actual events. Past events are different from events that are repeatable and observable. The scientific method is limited to that which can be tested, reproduced, and verified or falsified. That which lies outside of these parameters is not the same kind of science and requires some measure of faith about certain past conditions. Either humanistic naturalism or the revelation of creation can form the basis for assumptions about the past.

Science can test an assumption by evaluating the accuracy of the predictions of the different models. The model (or theory or belief or revelation) that best predicts that which is observable is the more credible model of reality. However, new observations cannot be directly made about past events, so verification is limited.

If a scientist brings wrong assumptions to the study of origins, the evidence can be obscured.

The laws of science require a Creator.

The universe has been created with very special scientific laws that enable us to live and to learn about them. The laws of nature do not have a naturalistic cause. The laws of nature did not cause the laws of nature.

> The miracle of the appropriateness of the language of mathematics for the formulation of the laws of physics is a wonderful gift which we neither understand nor deserve.[2]

We can see an objective mathematical structure in the physical universe. For example, consider the relationship of the periodic table and mathematics. One element is distinguished from another by the number of electrons, neutrons, and protons.

> How can it be that mathematics, being after all a product of human thought which is independent of experience, is so admirably appropriate to the objects of reality?[3]

Human Conscience

Regardless of cultural norms, humans all over the world have an innate sense of good and evil that demonstrates God's design in us. Everyone is given a sense of morality. We were created to love our Creator and to love one another. We experience guilt when we do not.

All men know that good is better than evil.

All societies claim to try to suppress evil and promote good. Kindness and care for family members, especially for children, are universal traits. Compassion for the elderly, poor, and weak are qualities valued by cultures around the world. Our consciences teach us that might does not make right. Instead, we know that might should choose to do right. This reflects our God-given command to care for each other.

A naturalistic model of origins would not predict socially established actions, such as care and kindness, actions that every culture recognizes as good. Selfish and cruel use of force—survival of the fittest—is routinely condemned, not praised.

All men acknowledge a spiritual part of life.

All societies are permeated with religious worship or at least sensitivity to spiritual things. Somehow what is spiritual is connected to our conscience. Every culture differs, but each one displays an interest in knowing and honoring God—or a religious disposition to substitute someone or something else in God's place.

There is a universal desire to know and be known by God or a substitute for Him. Likewise, there is a worldwide hunger to be rescued from moral failures and misbehaviors as well as a serious concern for what happens after we die.

All men recognize human authority over earth and its animals.

All societies demonstrate and understand that humans dominate the earth, ruling over animals, plant life, and the physical environment. All cultures have acknowledged the superiority of man over all other animate life, life forms, and inanimate objects in nature, as reflected in God's mandate for mankind to exercise dominion (Genesis 1:28).

Man's authority over animals, plants, and the rest of the earth has changed history through the use and consumption of animals (including herding livestock, riding horses, and fishing) and plants (such as using timber for building and crops for food) as well as the physical environment (diverting river water for irrigation, harnessing wind power for sailing and windmills, using rocks for buildings, and so on).

In addition, all societies have a spoken language of abstract thought and concepts. Human communication is very different from anything observed in animals. Why? Mankind knows he is the proper creature fit to rule the earth. This makes sense only if man was created to be morally superior to animals, plants, and the earth.

The Holy War

> Now Diabolus thought he was safe because he had cap-
> tured Mansoul and garrisoned himself within the city…
> He had spoiled the old law books and promoted his own
> vain lies. He had appointed new magistrates and set up
> new aldermen. He had built new strongholds and manned
> them with his own gang. He did all this to make himself
> secure in case the good Shaddai or his Son should try to
> invade the town.[4]

Much effort and vast amounts of capital have been spent attack-
ing the symptoms of a deeply imbedded sickness in modern society. In
every realm, whether political, educational, business, or religious, lead-
ership has concentrated on methods and processes to cure sociological or functional ills.

Much of the argument among politicians is over the cures for the
problems that plague us. But this argument is about treating the symptoms, not discovering the cause of the disease. We have reduced the
issues of human relationships to meaningless debates over techniques,
programs, and economic distribution. We have downgraded the universal human search for meaning to nothing more than a fulfilling self-
image. We have encoded the Darwinian survival of the fittest with the
New Age jargon of empowerment: "Be all you can be."

In biblical terms, the disease is sin, curable only by regeneration
through the work of the Holy Spirit made possible by the love of God
the Father expressed in the substitutional death, burial, and resurrection of the Lord Jesus Christ. In human terms, the disease is a naturalistic worldview, curable only by embracing a theistic worldview that
acknowledges the Creator.

The clearest contrast of the worldviews can be seen in the language
and perspectives commonly used to shape social mores. The radical
shift in morals and ethics seen in most countries may best be understood when contrasting today's naturalistic framework with the biblical perspective.

Prior to the sixteenth century, the two competing worldviews were supernatural belief systems. The biblical worldview is monotheistic and creationist, while the Babylonian and the subsequent Persian, Asian, Greek, and Roman cosmologies are either pantheistic or polytheistic but completely evolutionary. The early evolutionary religions worshipped either the individual personifications of natural forces (polytheism) or nature itself (pantheism).

The three monotheistic religions of the world (Judaism, Christianity, and Islam) are (or were) creationist at their core. All other religions, derived in some measure from the Babylonian worship of the forces of nature, are or were evolutionary. These two worldviews (or belief systems) now stand at the center of reflective and deductive thought.

The naturalist believes that there is no supernatural force in existence and that man is now able to direct the evolutionary development of the universe. The creationist believes that the Creator God exists and that His creatures must seek to understand His will.

The common data that both share will be interpreted in the light of the interpreter's belief system (or worldview, or faith). When we ask the questions that plague our minds—Why is the world full of evil? Why can't we all get along? Why can't we seem to get enough?—the answers come from our worldview.

The battle now being waged among the power centers of the world is essentially a strategic warfare guided by two entirely different belief systems. One seeks to control the affairs of men based on a naturalistic and humanistic worldview, and the other seeks to present a theistic and creationist worldview. The war between these worldviews constitutes the basis for mankind's opposing philosophies, religions, political platforms, and sociological tenets.

What we believe will frame our reactions, our priorities, and our expectations.

Desire for Justice

Humans in general, regardless of our cultural upbringings, naturally dislike injustice and naturally desire to see justice served.

The universal desire for equal justice (and just laws) demonstrates mankind's moral nature: Man (male and female) is a unique creature, created in God's image. Evolutionary theory postulates that man is an animal, different from other animals only in degree, not kind. But mankind's innate desire for justice is a proof of mankind's inherently moral nature, which itself is a proof of God's status as Creator.

Equal justice requires universal laws.

Real justice is equal. Equal justice requires universal laws. But universal laws do not emerge randomly; they need a universal Lawgiver. As a matter of moral justice, crimes and other types of social wrongdoing require a just consequence.

Although the details of each wrongdoing vary and should be balanced and weighed against relevant circumstances, real justice is ultimately equal to the offense committed (or else it is not truly just). Yet equal justice, whether penal or compensatory, requires universal laws in order to achieve equality in application.

Universal laws don't emerge randomly or by accident. Universal laws and equal justice must come from a universal and just Lawgiver—God Himself.

> Universal laws and equal justice must come from a universal and just Lawgiver—God Himself.

When our desire for equal justice through the application of universal laws is frustrated, this frustration is an indication of our sense that there is a Lawgiver (and Judge) above and beyond any society or culture. People throughout history have held the expectation that they will be judged after death. They intuitively recognize injustices in this life, they expect all injustices to be resolved hereafter by a truly equal justice, and they sense that this equal justice is based on God's universal laws.

Just laws rely on truth.

Laws based on falsehood or wrong are not just laws. Just laws must be based on what is true and what is right. Societies need to apply just laws in order to resolve social disputes and problems. Personal rights, valuable relationships, and social responsibilities are at stake. Therefore, the legal system needs to recognize and uphold the true and the right while rejecting the false and the wrong.

But to enforce just laws, we must be able to distinguish truth from falsehood and right from wrong. Does such a standard exist?

One objective moral standard is the Golden Rule—the standard of evaluating our own actions as just or unjust based on whether we would want those same actions to be done to us. This is a type of universal law that is "written in [our] hearts" (Romans 2:15). Slanderers don't think it right when they themselves are slandered. Likewise, thieves don't feel right about their own property being stolen. And cannibals certainly don't want to be eaten by their neighbors!

Reliable evidence is required.

To have justice, we need just laws. But just laws cannot work apart from true evidence, which is necessary for us to recognize what is relevant and true. Analyzing evidence requires recognizing relevance and testing for truth. Just laws rely on truth and right. But to recognize truth and right, we need reliable evidence to show what is true and right. (Sometimes this can be meaningfully corroborated by disproving something as false or wrong.)

Over the past centuries, the search for truth in science has been formalized into the scientific method, whereby theories are developed and tested according to a generally accepted standard. In a similar fashion, the legal profession operates by what is known as the rules of evidence. The idea of an orderly process for scrutinizing and testing something offered as evidence, when properly submitted for examination and cross-examination, underlies the logic of these rules of evidence.

God's Holiness Demands a Perfect Creation

> Holy, holy, holy, Lord God Almighty…Thou art worthy, O Lord, to receive glory and honor and power: for thou hast created all things, and for thy pleasure they are and were created (Revelation 4:8,11).

The holiness of God drives and limits His revelation of Himself to

His creation. Scripture is consistent. Holiness is God's fundamental nature, and that unique nature so permeates what God is and does that no action or thought from the Godhead can override it. The majestic seraphs so tantalizingly described in Isaiah 6 and Ezekiel 1—those four unique "living creatures" standing in the presence of the Creator (Revelation 4)— continually speak of the thrice-holy nature of God as they breathe.

Humanity will never know complete holiness until we see the new heavens and the new earth. We may well experience righteousness in our lifetimes as our hearts long for the presence of the holy God, but God's holiness—God's perfection—can only be believed.

God's holiness demands that only God can be the source of truth.

Because God is holy, He cannot lie (Hebrews 6:18), and whenever God reveals anything, He must reveal the truth about Himself and His nature. The Creator God is truth (John 14:6), and the originator of lies is the archenemy, Lucifer (John 8:44). Lies, even though they may contain partial truth, are the active agents that oppose God's truth as it is revealed to His creation.

This, of course, is the crux of all rebellion against God.

- Lies oppose the revelation of truth in the created things (the universe).

- Lies oppose the revelation of truth in the written Word (Scripture).

- Lies oppose the revelation of truth in the new creation (salvation).

Whenever partial truth is presented as *the* truth, whether the truth is mixed with error or is merely incomplete, that partial presentation is a lie. The Bible is very clear in this message: "God is light [truth], and in him is no darkness [lie, untruth] at all" (1 John 1:5). That biblical axiom is true whether applied to scientific research, educational philosophy, theological speculation, or heretical doctrine. Jesus Himself laid claim to that absolute when He said, "I am the way, the truth, and the life" (John 14:6).

God's holiness demands that He is and does truth.

The Creator God must reveal truth and cannot be untrue. When God speaks, He must speak truth. When God acts, He cannot commit error. One of the titles by which Jesus Christ is eternally known is Faithful and True (Revelation 19:11). God's holiness demands that the creation does not distort anything about God or about itself.

God could not create a lie—He could not make anything that would inexorably lead us to a wrong conclusion. Nor could He create processes that would counter His own nature or that would lead us to conclude something untrue about Him.

Evolutionary mechanisms are, by their very nature, random and nonfunctional. Nothing in naturalist theory directs evolution. Vast eons of chaos, with death weeding out the ineffective, are thought to somehow produce processes and systems of apparent design. No god in this system exists to create anything.

Christians who seek to harmonize the biblical revelation of a holy God with the antithetical evolutionary theories are constructing dangerous hybrids that blaspheme the very God they insist they believe in. May God protect us from such thinking.

Summarizing the Evidence

Natural laws. Scientific models are attempts to accurately correlate understanding to the way things really are. Thus, science is not possible without a truthful reality to model.

Human conscience. All people live according to moral laws, regardless of whether they verbally admit it.

Desire for justice. Even those who deny moral laws inadvertently admit that moral laws are real whenever they verbally object to having been wronged.

Biblical Insight

Romans 2:14-16 describes the human conscience. The conscience is an innate knowledge of moral laws. Moral laws are prescriptions for behavior. A conscience identifies wrongdoing, either before or after the act.

1. Has any moral law ever come from anything but a person?

2. Try to summarize the logical argument Paul makes in this passage.

3. Paul states that even those people who have no knowledge of Scripture (the law) nevertheless have been given enough legal knowledge for them to be accountable at judgment day. According to Romans 1, what other witness sufficient to judgment has God provided for all men?

3

Evidence from Nature

*The heavens declare the glory of God; and the firmament
showeth his handiwork. Day unto day uttereth
speech, and night unto night showeth knowledge.*

Psalm 19:1-2

*It seems as though somebody has fine-tuned nature's numbers to
make the Universe... The impression of design is overwhelming.*

Paul Davies

Nature Is God's Language for all Humanity

The evidence for creation can be clearly seen from that which has been made by our Creator. Our planet has been uniquely created by God for life, especially human life. Our universe is filled with wonder that demonstrates our wonderful Creator. Through what was made we can see God's power, presence, protection, provision, and wisdom. Nature eloquently testifies to an infinite, eternal, omnipotent, omniscient, living, personal God.

Nature reveals God's power.

The awesome power of our Creator is seen throughout the universe. Even a child can see stars at night. But who has the power necessary to put them there?

A small reflection of the power of our Creator is seen in the thousands of stars that shine in the night sky. Galaxies consist of millions of stars packed close together. And billions of galaxies fill the universe. If we took the time to look up at night and think about the amount of power displayed in the heavens, we would be overwhelmed. This reveals God's power at the cosmic level.

Everyone can appreciate the power of the sun. The sun lights our days so we can see nature all around us. (Even a blind person can feel the warmth of the sun.) Our sun and other stars are bright because they radiate energy, both visible and invisible. Some of this energy radiating from the sun is needed, directly or indirectly, to power all life forms on earth. Some of the other energy, also very powerful, is harmful to life.

The energy that is useful to life is a very small part of the spectrum. It is the part that we can see. Due to the laws of physics established by our Creator, visible light is the best energy for the chemical reactions of life. Unlike high-energy radiation, such as X-rays and gamma rays (which harm living cells), visible light enables human eyes to see, and it powers plant growth, the foundation of all food chains on earth. Even the energetic behavior of little bugs ultimately depends on the power of the sun.

God's power extends from wonders great and small that we can observe in our awesome universe, including the sun and stars (which look small to us yet are actually huge).

The study of power is called thermodynamics. That term is a compound of two Greek words, *therme* ("heat") and *dunamis* ("power"). It is the science that speaks of the power or energy contained in heat and its conversion to other forms of energy. The term *energy* is itself derived from the Greek word *energeia* ("working") and is normally defined as "the capacity to do work." In modern scientific terminology, *energy* and *work* are considered equivalent. Something that has energy has the capacity to do work—that is, the capacity to exert a force through a distance.

Power is closely related to energy. Power is the work done, or the energy expended to do the work, per unit of time. It is measured in foot-pounds per second.

All processes are fundamentally energy-conversion processes, and everything that happens in the physical universe is a process of some kind, so the study of thermodynamics is recognized as the most universal and fundamental of all science. Everything that exists in the universe is some form of energy, and every natural thing that happens is some form of energy conversion.

No energy can be created now because only God can create energy, and God has "rested from all his work which God created and made" (Genesis 2:3). Energy cannot be destroyed because He is now "upholding all things by the word of his power" (Hebrews 1:3). "I know that, whatsoever God doeth, it shall be for ever: nothing can be put to it, nor any thing taken from it" (Ecclesiastes 3:14).

> No energy can be created now because
> only God can create energy.

Nature reveals God's presence.

The presence of God is evident everywhere—in the immensity of the universe and at levels too small for the human eye to see. The Bible teaches that the universe is as infinitely great as the very thoughts and ways of God (Isaiah 55:9) and that it will endure forever (Psalm 148:1-6; Daniel 12:3; Ecclesiastes 3:14). We can study it and describe it and serve in it eternally without ever exhausting its infinite beauties and mysteries.

God's presence can be detected even in the most commonplace substances, such as water. Our physical bodies are mostly water! God provides the water for life. Our planet is close enough to the sun to provide the water necessary for life. If it were just a little farther from the sun, all that water would become ice!

Water itself is a very small molecule (just a three-atom unit of hydrogen and oxygen), but it is the primary ingredient of our planet (that is, earth's biggest component). God's design of the behavior of water molecules and the impact water has on our entire planet are examples of His creative design and custodial presence on the smallest and largest scales.

Water expands when it freezes, unlike most other substances. Ice and snow take up more volume than the same amount of liquid water.

This makes water denser as a liquid than it is when frozen, so ice floats. If ice did not float on the surface of water, the floors of the oceans and lakes would be covered with glaciers of ice that would never melt. Surface ice also helps regulate the climate by reflecting energy.

As a liquid, water's temperature range is perfect for cycling water from the oceans to the land. Water requires a lot of energy to evaporate into a vapor, and it releases this energy when it condenses back into liquid. This balances temperatures in the earth's climate and inside living cells. If less energy were required for evaporation, then streams, rivers, and lakes would evaporate away quickly.

Beautiful clouds and sunsets inspire praise for the Creator who forms them. Because God's creative presence is shown in even commonplace yet needful things, we are blessed by the huge quantities of water that flow though our biosphere.

Nature reveals God's protection.

Life itself is fragile, yet God's protection can be seen in the careful design of our physical environment. Our bodies need many forms of protection from exotic dangers, such as rocks falling from space, and from the mundane dangers, such as temperature extremes.

If our earth had a thinner atmosphere, our planet would be hit with lethal amounts of incoming rocks and harmful radiation. Mercury, Pluto, and the moon have almost no air at all. Their surfaces are scarred with craters from the impacts of giant boulders, little pebbles, and small grains of sand. The surfaces of these planets are very hot when facing the sun and very cold when facing away. If earth had a thicker atmosphere, our planet would be boiling hot. The atmospheres on Venus and the "gas giant" planets (Jupiter, Saturn, Uranus, and Neptune) are very heavy. On Venus, for instance, the surface pressure is 90 times that of earth! The surface pressures of Jupiter, Saturn, Uranus, and Neptune are even higher.

Earth has just the right mixture of nitrogen and oxygen in its atmosphere. Venus and the gas giants have the wrong kind of gases for humans (or any other life forms) to survive there. Venus is mostly carbon dioxide. The gas giants are mostly hydrogen and helium. The other planets have little or no "air" at all. Truly, the very air we breathe is an invisible yet universal witness to God's protective providence.

Sunlight reaches us through our transparent atmosphere. Even though we can see through the atmosphere, it functions as a filter. It lets in the sun's radiation that is useful to life, but it blocks most of the radiation that is harmful to life. Only a fraction of the radio waves and some of the visible light and infrared radiations are blocked, but almost all of the harmful ultraviolet rays, X-rays, and gamma rays never reach us.

We have been given an atmosphere that protects us. It provides just the right amount of air and warmth we need. It allows the sunlight to reach the plants that feed us. Our transparent atmosphere not only protects us but also allows us to the see the stars and wonders of the heavens. The question is, are these marvelous devices merely accidents, or are they evidence of incredible design by a Creator?

Design in living things is obvious. Even a single-celled organism is too complex for scientists to understand, let alone duplicate. All of life is governed by the marvelously complex genetic code, which contains not only design and order but also the equivalent of written information. This DNA code must be written correctly, and the rest of the cell must be able to read it and follow its instructions if the cell is to metabolize its food, carry out the myriad of enzyme reactions, and reproduce. This code had to be present at the origin of life.

> Even a single-celled organism is too complex for scientists to understand, let alone duplicate.

The human eye gives obvious evidence of design. With its many functioning parts—the lens, cornea, and iris; the controlling muscles; the sensitive rods and cones, which translate light energy into chemical signals; the optic nerve, which speeds these signals to a decoding center in the brain; and on and on—the eye was unquestionably designed by an incredibly intelligent Designer who had a complete grasp of optical physics.

The list is endless. God has provided overwhelming evidence of His care in the design of our universe, our earth, all living things…and especially humans. Everything everywhere bears the fingerprints of an omniscient Designer who loves and cares for His creation.

Nature reveals God's provision.

Our Creator provides every good thing in nature that is needful or useful for humans or other creatures. God provides everything we need. Consider this: Why does the earth provide edible food in the first place? If the planting and harvesting of crops were not so commonplace, we would (or should) regard the growing cycles of corn, beans, fruit trees, potatoes, or any other plant as amazing miracles.

The sun's energy warms our planet. Hot air blows from areas heated by the sun to cooler areas. The sun's energy brings rain. Water evaporates from the ocean and falls to the land as it cools. The sun powers the winds that move the water vapor to the land. The sun's energy renews the air. With our sun's energy, plants convert carbon dioxide into oxygen. The sun's energy grows food. Plants capture sunlight and store it in sugar, starch, and fat.

OZONE, THE GEOMAGNETIC FIELD, AND CELL MEMBRANES: GOD'S PROTECTION

An entire list of protective features is required for living things to survive. Thus, the protection of life is an all-or-nothing system. All-or-nothing systems are always and only generated by persons, so the all-or-nothing life-protection system had to have been generated by the person of God.

Ozone is required for life on earth even though it is extremely toxic to living tissues! It is a unique molecule made of three oxygen atoms, and it blankets earth's upper atmosphere, where it does not interact with living tissues far below. However, it filters out the sun's ultraviolet (UV) blast of radiation. Without ozone, UV light would damage so much DNA that life would quickly end.

Similarly, the earth harbors a magnetic field that is strong enough to shield earth but not so strong that it would disrupt chemical reactions in living cells. It extends into space, intercepting charged particles that strike earth. The particles are extremely chemically reactive, bare atomic nuclei mostly emitted from solar flares. When they are caught by the earth's magnetic field, they become visible "auroras." These particles would quickly poison life if they were permitted to penetrate earth's surface.

Ozone, UV light, charged particles, too much magnetic field strength, and even water all disrupt the molecules of life: DNA and proteins. Thus, ozone is positioned far up in the sky away from life, UV light is kept from life by that very ozone, the geomagnetic field is the right strength for life, and cells have membranes that help retain just the right amounts of water inside them. In fact, tiny, ingenious pumping motors made of protein molecules, coordinated with molecular signals and switches, constantly regulate the water level in every cell.

Only our God, the Lord Jesus Christ, could have put all these protections in place, all at one time!

Many other stars are too hot to support life. Many are too cold. Some vary from hot to cold too much. Some stars are too big, and some are too small. Our sun is one of the few ideally suited to support life. It has the right brightness and variability. It radiates the right range of energy in the right amounts. Most stars in the universe are not perfectly balanced for life, but our sun is.

There are thousands of examples of an integrated and purposeful plan for provision throughout the flora and fauna of our planet. Everywhere you look, if you really try to understand what is going on, you can easily see an intelligent Designer behind the common, everyday occurrences of our world.

Bread in one form or another is beyond question the most basic form of food in practically every human society, past or present—so much so that it is often called "the staff of life." Fossilized cakes of bread have even been found in a number of ancient archaeological sites.

That ordinary food, so common throughout the world, has been made from many different kinds of grain. The wheat or barley or other grain is ground into flour, mixed with water, and baked into cakes or loaves. Various other ingredients are often added to produce different varieties of bread, but bread almost inevitably becomes the most essential foodstuff of a society.

At one time, God's chosen people had to live in a hostile desert environment for 40 years and could neither plant grain nor produce bread. In answer to their prayers, however, God "satisfied them with the bread of heaven" (Psalm 105:40). That was the wonderful manna, which miraculously appeared on the ground each day in the wilderness. The manna was actually called "the corn of heaven" and "angels' food" (Psalm 78:24-25).

Whether a unique provision like manna or an ordinary provision through the growth of grain (which we often take for granted), God provides it all, "for he maketh his sun to rise on the evil and on the good, and sendeth rain on the just and on the unjust" (Matthew 5:45).

Nature reveals God's wisdom.

The wisdom and cleverness of our Creator is seen in the orderly structure and complexity of life and the systems that demonstrate intelligence while supporting that life. Wisdom enables us to understand reality. Through wisdom we have discovered a set of scientific laws that elegantly express reality in the language of mathematics. As we have seen, whenever man learns the logic of the universe, man is (in essence) "thinking God's thoughts after Him." We humans discover and implement wisdom; we do not invent it.

In particular, the beginning and sustaining of our universe are dynamic displays of the Creator's wisdom, some of which we can scientifically discover and understand. When we do, we feel as if we are walking in the footprints of someone who previously walked through a snowdrift.

The unfathomable amount of applied knowledge (wisdom) that was used to invent the universe and to preprogram its interactive workings is a source of wonder beyond the imagination. In light of the stupendous power and quantity displayed in the heavens, David the psalmist asked God, "What is man, that thou art mindful of him?" (Psalm 8:4).

How could a creature such as a human begin to comprehend the wisdom built into the interactive universe? As we saw in chapter 1, the very fact that humans have any wisdom at all, not to mention the wisdom necessary to understand a meaningful amount of the workings of the universe, is more amazing than the marvelous physics of the universe itself! How can an immaterial mind, residing inside a human body made mostly of water (along with other elements of the earth), comprehend anything?

As we noted in that chapter, only by God's creative grace can we humans think any thoughts at all, much less thoughts that are logical and analytical enough to be considered scientific. God's wisdom is displayed in the universe itself and in our human ability to comprehend that universe, so we owe our great Creator-God an ongoing debt of creaturely thanksgiving.

No one can scientifically prove that the animal or human brain was not created by a Supreme Intelligence. The question of origins—creation or evolution—is almost entirely outside the experimental domain of science, for when the first brain was formed, there were no human observers. Cognitively, however, and from observation, we can reasonably conclude that the human brain was created.

If we choose to believe that we are the product of chance and random processes (evolution) and that man is perhaps merely the highest order of animal, we will possess a materialistic and relativistic philosophy. On the other hand, if we choose to believe that our brain was created by a Master Intelligence, we will have a theological worldview, one which should prompt us to use our minds to understand God's purpose for His creation.

Natural Revelation

> The invisible things of him from the creation of the world are clearly seen, being understood by the things that are made, even his eternal power and Godhead; so that they are without excuse (Romans 1:20).

There has been much discussion about the amount and quality of the natural revelation God has displayed in the universe He created. Much has been discovered about the processes and functioning of our world—so much that some have suggested that these facts of science must be used to interpret the written text of Scripture.

How do the "things that are made" help us understand God's truth?

The written words of Scripture are inspired, and it is clear from passages like Psalm 19:1-4 and Romans 1:18-20 that God created the universe to "speak," "declare," and "show" much of His nature. It follows then that the creation itself would make "clearly seen" that which can be understood about the Creator—unless there is a willing rebellion against that truth (Romans 1:21-25).

The creation declares and speaks of God's glory, but the "law of the LORD is perfect...the testimony of the LORD is sure...The statutes of the LORD are right" (Psalm 19:7-8). Created things tell us something about the nature of God, but the revealed words define, clarify, limit, and command. The writings (the Scriptures) are inspired (or more literally, "God-breathed"), as Paul reminds us in 2 Timothy 3:16-17.

Natural revelation, therefore, provides only limited insight into truth. Final authority rests in the written revelation that God "breathed" into a living record (1 Peter 1:23) that "shall not pass away" (Mark 13:31). We can understand the events of creation only by revelation, not by discovery. Science cannot duplicate or comprehend creation. Man can merely steward that which is preserved by the Creator in His patient mercy (2 Peter 3:8-9).

What we believe about the creation, we believe about the Savior.

Jesus Christ is clearly both Creator and Savior. Such passages as John 1:1-14, Colossians 1:16-19, and Hebrews 1:1-3 manifestly declare that Jesus, the Word made flesh, is none other than our Lord and Creator. What is revealed to us about the nature of the Creator teaches us about the nature of the Savior. The Gospel points us to "worship him that made heaven, and earth, and the sea, and the fountains of waters" (Revelation 14:7).

The doctrine of creation cannot be separated from the doctrine of salvation. Only the omnipotent, omniscient, omnipresent Creator could accomplish the work of redemption on Calvary, implementing an eternal reconciliation of all things to the immutable will and purpose of the Creator-Redeemer.

Scripture reveals that the creation demonstrates the nature of the Creator, so the inextricably bound attributes of the Father, Son, and Spirit cannot be in conflict with the message of the created things. Nor can the message of the gospel conflict with the message discovered in the creation. God cannot lie (Titus 1:2) by word or by action.

Creation issues are foundational to a biblical worldview.

The gospel we present must include "all the counsel of God" (Acts 20:27). The secular worldview is in direct opposition to a Creator. It knows and acknowledges nothing of the need for eternal redemption. It speaks only of self-centered appeasement. Naturalism at its core is atheistic, and the thrust of evolutionary theory is to tell the story of our origins without God.

We who have been given the high privilege of being "ambassadors for Christ" (2 Corinthians 5:20) must ensure that our teachings about the creation, the dominion mandate, the fall of man, and the plan of redemption are as accurate as our human minds can portray, guided by and submitted to the revealed words of our Creator.

Evidence from the Earth

Secularists like to consider earth as just one of many millions of planets, occupying an obscure place in an insignificant galaxy in a sea of nothingness. The Bible teaches, however, that earth is very special to the Creator, performing a crucial role in the universe today and being prepared for an unending role in the cosmic saga.

Earth is the location God chose to situate His image in man after He had created everything in wisdom. This is where God sent His only begotten Son to live a perfect life and die a sufficient sacrifice once man had rejected Him. It is also special in a temporal sense, well-designed for man's habitation. God created it in an orderly fashion, with each step necessary for the life and well-being of man.

As far as science knows, planet earth is unique in the entire universe. Certainly this is true in our own solar system. Nothing we have observed leads us to believe that there is any other planet like earth.

The earth is perfectly designed.

A brief glance at the earth compared to all other known planets reveals many contrasts. Even from outer space, the earth stands in stark contrast to the other seven planets in our solar system. Earth is the only planet circling our sun on which life as we know it could exist.

Like no other planet, ours is covered with green vegetation, enormous blue-green oceans containing more than a million islands, hundreds of thousands of streams and rivers, huge land masses, mountains, ice caps, and deserts that produce a spectacular variety of color and texture. Some form of life is found in virtually every ecological niche on the earth's surface. Even in the extremely cold Antarctica, hardy microscopic beings thrive in ponds, tiny wingless insects live in patches of moss and lichen, and plants grow and flower yearly. From the apex of the atmosphere to the bottom of the oceans, from the coldest part of the poles to the warmest part of the equator, life thrives here. No evidence of life has been found on any other planet.

The earth is immense, about 8000 miles in diameter, with a mass calculated at roughly 6.6×10^{21} (6.6 sextillion) tons. The earth is an average of 93 million miles from the sun. If the earth traveled much faster in its 584-million-mile journey around the sun, its orbit would become larger and it would move farther away from the sun. If it moved too far from this narrow habitable zone, all life would cease to exist on earth. If it traveled slightly slower in its orbit, the earth would move closer to the sun, and if it moved too close, all life would likewise perish. The earth's trip around the sun takes 365 days, 6 hours, 49 minutes, and 9.54 seconds (the sidereal year) and is consistent to more than a thousandth of a second!

If the yearly average temperature on earth's surface changed by only a few degrees or so, much of the life on it would eventually roast or freeze. This change would upset the water-to-ice ratio and other critical balances with disastrous results. If the earth rotated slower on its axis, all life would die in time, either by freezing at night because of lack of heat from the sun or by burning during the day from too much heat.

> If the earth rotated slower on its axis, all life would die in time.

Our normal earth processes are assuredly unique among our solar system and, as far as we know, in the entire universe.

The sun and moon are perfectly designed.

Of all the energy the sun gives off, only 0.45 billionth of its daily output strikes the earth. The sun provides the earth with energy estimated at more than 239 trillion horsepower, or about 35,000 horsepower for each current resident. Even though several hundred billion galaxies likely exist in the universe, each with 100 billion stars, there is only one atom for every 88 gallons of space, which means the vast majority of the universe is empty space!

Our sun belongs to a spectral class representing only 5 percent of all stars: G2V (also called *yellow dwarf* or *main sequence*). It is also called a variable star because it pulsates in size and brightness. Many in this class pulsate much more radically than the sun, giving off deadly flares. Some flares and coronal mass ejections have topped the charts in recent years. The energy of these magnetic storms escapes between the granules instead of heating the photosphere. As a result, the sun's heat output, or solar constant, has only varied by .06 of 1 percent during the entire observational period of 1974–2006.

How does our sun compare with its classmates? In one of the longest-running observational programs of the twentieth century, researchers White, Wallace, and Livingstone published the results of their "Sun as a Star" program in the *Astrophysical Journal*. This data set spanning 32 years—a rarity in science—concluded that our sun is uncommonly stable.

The sun is a star among countless others, but in many respects it stands alone. It is the perfect lighthouse for the one planet that we know harbors life. Rejoicing like "a strong man to run a race," it journeys across our sky each day, radiating its life-sustaining energy and declaring the glory of God (Psalm 19:1-6).

If the moon were much larger or nearer to the earth, the huge tides that would result would overflow onto the lowlands and erode the mountains. If the continents were leveled, the entire surface of the earth would be covered with water a mile deep! If the earth were not tilted 23 degrees on its axis, but rather was on a 90-degree angle in reference to the sun, we would not have four seasons.

Without seasons, life would soon not be able to exist on earth—the poles would lie in eternal twilight, and water vapor from the oceans would be carried by the wind toward both the north and south, freezing when it moved close enough to the poles. In time, huge continents of snow and ice would pile up in the polar regions, leaving most of the earth a dry desert. The oceans would eventually disappear, and rainfall would cease. The accumulated weight of ice at the poles would cause the equator to bulge, and, as a result, the earth's rotation would drastically change.

Just a little change (in the perspective of the universe) would render the earth unsuitable to support any life. Is this the result of accidental randomness or purposeful intent?

The cycle of water is perfectly designed.

What makes the earth so beautiful? Interplay between the light from the sun and the white, blue, green, and brown colors from the earth produce incredible vistas from mountaintops and space. The ocean and atmosphere, the grasses and forests, the mountains and deserts, and the clouds and snow reflect, absorb, and scatter various colors of the rainbow.

The earth is the only planet known to have huge bodies of water. Seventy percent of its surface area consists of oceans, lakes, and rivers. The few planets that have water contain only moisture floating as vapor on their surface or small amounts of ice or liquid on the planet itself, not large bodies of liquid water as on earth.

Liquid water is necessary for most life processes on the earth and explains why the planet is so fertile. Some of the other planets, such as Mars, may have contained liquid water in the past as evidenced by erosional features, but this water has evaporated and escaped into space, or it is trapped in the crust in frozen form.

Water is unique in that it can absorb enormous amounts of heat without a large alteration in its temperature. Its heat absorption level is about ten times as great as steel. During the day, the earth's bodies of water rapidly soak up enormous amounts of heat, so the earth stays fairly cool. At night, they release the vast amounts of heat they absorbed during the day, which, combined with atmospheric effects, keeps most of the surface from freezing solid at night. If it were not for the tremendous amounts of water on the earth, far greater day and night temperature variations would exist. Many parts of the surface would be hot enough to boil water during the day and cold enough to freeze water at night. Because water is an excellent temperature stabilizer, the large oceans on earth are vital for life to exist on earth.

In contrast to virtually all other materials (the rare exceptions include rubber and antimony), water contracts when cooled only until it reaches four degrees Celsius. Then, amazingly, it expands until it freezes. Because of this anomaly, the ice that forms in seas, oceans, and lakes stays near the surface, where the sun heats it during the day and the warm water below melts it in the summer. This and the Coriolis effect, which produces ocean currents, ensure that most of the ocean stays in a liquid form, allowing the myriad of water creatures to live.

This is one more stunning demonstration that the "LORD by wisdom hath founded the earth; by understanding hath he established the heavens" (Proverbs 3:19). These unique features, all working together to form the properties of this most basic of life-supporting compounds, cannot justly be called "coincidences" or "random accumulations." Water is a created necessity to our planet and to our life.

The atmosphere is perfectly designed.

The mixture of gases usually found in the atmosphere not contaminated by human pollution is perfect for life. If it were much different (for example, if it had 17 percent oxygen instead of 21 percent, or if it had too little carbon dioxide, or if the atmospheric pressure were much higher or lower), life would cease to exist on earth.

The air close to the earth's surface is heated by light energy from the sun, and after the air is warmed it becomes less dense and rises upward. The result is that the air near the earth's surface maintains a temperature in which life can exist. If air contracted when heated and became denser, the temperature on the earth's surface would become unbearable, and most life could not survive for very long. The temperature a few hundred feet above the surface, on the other hand, would be extremely cold, and most life could also not exist there for very long. The only habitable region would be a thin slice of air, but even here life could not exist for long because the plants and trees necessary to support the life in the atmosphere could not survive, as they would be in the cold zone. Thus birds would have no resting place, nor would they have food, water, or oxygen. But because air on the earth's surface rises when heated, life can exist on the earth.

The movement of warm air from the surface rising upward creates air currents, which are important parts of the earth's ecological system. These currents (winds) carry away carbon dioxide from areas that overproduce it and move oxygen to areas that need it, such as the large urban population centers.

God has designed the atmosphere to maintain a uniform temperature, whether there is a cooling or a warming tendency. He created the atmosphere with a built-in thermostat that maintains thermal equilibrium.

If our atmosphere were much thinner, many of the millions of meteors that now are burned up would reach the earth's surface, causing death, destruction, and fires everywhere. The contrast becomes even greater when examining the atmospheres of our neighboring planets, Mars and Venus. Unlike earth, Mars has no global magnetic field. High-energy particles impacting a barrier generate showers of secondary particles, causing even more damage. Mars is no place for playful romps. Dust devils meandering over the ultra-dry surface generate highly oxidizing compounds, blanketing the soil with toxic chemicals and charging the dust with static electricity. Fine dust would get into everything, irritating moist membranes and damaging equipment. Mars probably smells awful too, and the atmosphere is so thin, nobody could hear you scream.

Venus is curiously similar to earth yet profoundly different. Venus has a sultry atmosphere, supersonic winds, a mountain higher than Everest, volcanic flows that look like pancakes, and about a thousand craters—but no plate tectonics and only a weak magnetic field. Our ideas about Venus have made an almost complete about-face since 1960, when many hoped it was a lush, tropical world that might host exotic life.

This hellish world now poses a serious challenge to uniformitarian views, which hold that slow, gradual changes over vast ages produced the geologic features we observe today. The opposing view, catastrophism, holds that many if not most of these features resulted from rapid, catastrophic events. Craters, mountains, and volcanic features all appear to be the same age. Planetary scientists, believing in long ages, have been forced to infer that the first 90 percent of the planet's history is missing![1]

Evolutionary naturalism is perplexed at what it finds on Mars and Venus—because such reasoning tries to determine how such conditions could come about naturally without catastrophic intervention. Such thinking is clouded by the restriction that God does not exist and that everything came about through random processes over eons of time.

Creationists, on the other hand, find the 90 percent of time missing on Venus and the unlivable thin atmosphere on Mars nothing more than continued evidence that "the heaven, even the heavens, are the LORD's: but the earth hath he given to the children of men" (Psalm 115:16).

Those who insist on an explanation that excludes God in their thinking will always be perplexed at what they discover. In the meantime, step outside underneath the gentle sun, breathe the sweet air, and thank God for His "wonderful works to the children of men" (Psalm 107:8).

The earth is a unique environment.

If evolution works to transform life to fit the existing environments, why has it not equally conquered all of the various environments here and elsewhere? Earth is the only planet circling our sun on which life as we know it could exist. A brief glance at the earth and all other known planets finds many startling contrasts. Like no other planet, ours is covered with green vegetation, blue-green seas, streams, rivers, mountains, and deserts that produce a spectacular variety of color and texture. All other known planets are covered with lifeless soil that varies only according to slight movements made by wind or mild air currents.

Earth is far better suited for life than any other planet, yet even here most of the environments are too hot, too cold, too far underground, or too far above ground to support much life. In the many thousands of miles of changing environments from the center of the earth to the edge of its atmosphere, there are only a few meters of habitable environment for most life forms, and therefore, almost all creatures are forced to live there. Although in our solar system only the earth was made to be inhabited (Isaiah 45:18), even on the earth only a thin slice is ideally suited for most life forms, including those we are most familiar with, such as mammals, birds, and reptiles.

> Earth is far better suited for life than any other planet.

This thin section, though, is teeming with life. It is estimated that an acre of typical farm soil, six inches deep, has several tons of living bacteria, almost a ton of fungi, 200 pounds of one-cell protozoan animals, about 100 pounds of yeast, and the same amount of algae.

The chances of a planet being just the right size, the proper distance away from the right star, and so on are extremely minute, even if many stars have planets circling them, as some speculate. The mathematical odds that all of these and other essential conditions happened by chance are astronomical—something like billions to one!

Three Creation Witnesses

We have suggested that the text of Scripture is more trustworthy than the theology of those who study it. Even though many godly scholars have made a genuine effort to understand and apply the words of God, every Christian is ultimately responsible to search the

Scriptures daily (Acts 17:11) to verify the teachings of men against the words of God's inspired writings.

Debates among biblically committed theologians and among godly pastors rarely have to do with salvation issues, the deity of Jesus Christ, or even the inspiration of Scripture. Usually these arguments are about bigger pictures, such as eschatology and ecclesiology. And yes, the meaning of the creation account is becoming one of the more heated debates among evangelicals.

Various hybrid theories about creation thrive among evangelicals. The *gap theory* was popularized in the early 1900s and is still embraced by some. Several iterations of the *day-age theory* are more common, with *progressive creation* widely held among academics. Then there are the literalists who accept the words of Genesis at face value and as actual history.

Although the Bible is clear that without faith it is impossible to please God (Hebrews 11:6), there is ample evidence that the Creator exists.

The universe itself (Romans 1:20) identifies His eternal power and triune nature. Creation becomes the universal "speech" and "language" of God to man about Himself (Psalm 19:1-3). The triune Godhead is certainly in view; and not only the Trinity but also the nature of that Godhead.

Human existence itself (Acts 17:28-29) demonstrates the eternal presence of the Creator God. This includes the innate knowledge present in all humanity but especially the powerful evidence of the new creation in believers (2 Corinthians 5:17; Ephesians 4:24).

The incarnation of the Lord Jesus, the Word made flesh (John 1:14; Philippians 2:5-9), incorporates the fullness of God (Colossians 2:9). Christ's life and ministry are vivid evidence of His omnipotence—especially the seven great miracles of creation recorded in the Gospel of John.

Thus, we have a threefold historical witness:

the "things that are made" (the universe)

humanity and the new birth

Jesus Christ—His life, word, and ministry

These revealed witnesses are progressively clearer and more accurate. The universe is designed to "speak" and "show" invisible things, but these must by their vastness be both difficult and mysterious to discern. The new creation of the salvation event is certainly more visible because the lifestyle and character of each individual should reflect a more visible righteousness. Those who are born again (John 3:3) are the "epistle of Christ" (2 Corinthians 3:3), God's "workmanship, created in Christ Jesus unto good works" (Ephesians 2:10).

The ultimate Truth, however, is the Lord Jesus Christ Himself (John 14:6) and His Word that He has given us (John 17:17). Jesus insisted that the miracles He performed while He was here on earth were enough proof—even if we have a hard time believing what He has said (John 10:38).

We may have difficulty seeing the invisible eternal power and Godhead from the evidence written into the very fabric of the universe, and we may see contradictions in the lives and testimonies of those who claim to participate in the "divine nature" (2 Peter 1:4). It is even possible to deny the reality of the historical record and witnesses of Christ's miracles. But the written record, the words of God, shall not pass away (Matthew 24:35), and those words have eternal life (John 6:68).

If we are unable to trust the words of God, we are surely doomed to wander in the ignorance of unbelief, "ever learning, and never able to come to the knowledge of the truth" (2 Timothy 3:7).

The Declaration of the Heavens

Our universe is filled with awesome wonders. There are billions of galaxies, each containing billions of stars, each one named by the Creator (Isaiah 40:26). Even the configurations of the stars in the heavens have a purpose (Job 38:31-33).

> The heavens declare the glory of God; and the firmament showeth his handiwork. Day unto day uttereth speech, and night unto night showeth knowledge (Psalm 19:1-2).

God is both omniscient and omnipotent. He has the wisdom to know what is best to do and the power to accomplish it. He makes no mistakes and never needs to go back and revise or redirect something He started. What He does is forever!

Many Scriptures (such as Psalm 148:1-6) assure us that the sun, moon, and stars, as well as the renewed earth, will continue to function through all the endless ages to come. Nothing can defeat God's primeval purposes in creating them. The Creator of the infinitely complex, highly energized cosmos must necessarily be omniscient and omnipotent. Having created life, as well as human personalities, He must also be a living person. No effect can be greater than its cause.

Therefore, God is fully capable of revealing to us knowledge about His creation—knowledge that could never be learned through studying present processes. It almost seems that He must do this, in fact, since He surely is not capricious. He would not create men and women who long to know the meaning of their lives, yet neglect or refuse to tell them anything about it.

Giant telescopes have only begun to reveal the immense numbers and fantastic variety of the stars. With literally billions of galaxies, and billions of stars in every galaxy, the number of the stars seems to be almost without limit. The variety is equally amazing—red giants, white dwarfs, Cepheid variables, neutron stars, pulsars, and on and on! As the Bible says in an amazing preview of modern astronomy, "There is one glory of the sun, and another glory of the moon, and another glory of the stars: for one star differeth from another star in glory" (1 Corinthians 15:41).

The idea of a simple fiat creation of the entire universe in its present form may seem too naive to evolutionary astronomers and cosmologists. Nevertheless, it fits all the facts of observational astronomy more easily and directly than does any other theory. The objection that special creation is not scientific because it is not observable is irrelevant because exactly the same objection applies to any of the evolutionary models. Who has ever observed a star evolve, or a "big bang," or an evolution of matter out of nothing?

There is much to "see" and to "hear" from the heavens. The universe writes the character of God with a broad sweep of His handwriting for all to know. One well-known Christian intellectual and apologist of

Jesus' day, the apostle Paul, wrote, "The invisible things of him from the creation of the world are clearly seen, being understood by the things that are made, even his eternal power and Godhead" (Romans 1:20). Paul then concludes that those who reject the "speech" and "language" of the universe are "without excuse."

> The universe writes the character of God with a broad sweep of His handwriting for all to know.

BLUE STARS TESTIFY TO A YOUNG UNIVERSE

Blue stars burn so brightly that they consume their fuel much faster than other stars. Blue stars should not exist in a universe that is billions of years old; they should have burned out billions of years ago. University of South Carolina astronomer Danny Faulkner recently noted, "In fact, the hottest blue stars could last only a few million years at best. Both creationists and evolutionists acknowledge this fact."[2]

Thus, long-age defenders suggest that new blue stars have been constantly generated over countless eons. But that means blue stars should be forming even now. "Despite their diligent search, however, [astronomers] have never observed one of these blue stars forming—or any other star, for that matter," Faulkner wrote.[3]

Stars cannot simply form from collapsing gases because the repulsive forces between each particle are far greater than their gravitational attraction. Thus, "It is not clear how blue stragglers form," according to long-age astronomers at NASA who reported the 2011 discovery of blue stars in the core of the Milky Way galaxy.[4] Blue stars, scattered throughout the universe, are considered "stragglers" because they appear to lag behind the aging process that supposedly made their redder-colored stellar peers older.

If these stars were products of nature and not God, a reasonable naturalistic explanation for their formation should be straightforward. But it is not. On the other hand, if the universe and its
stars are only thousands of years old, blue stars need no other
explanation. The scientific evidence shows, and the Bible clearly
states, that blue stars were put in place on purpose recently.

Each day tells us about God.

The "day unto day" faithfulness of constant stability and dependable processes is a "speech" without words that testifies to God's care
and provision.

We have touched on the wonders of the sun and the moon. These
great lights were obviously designed to "rule" the daytime and the
nighttime (Genesis 1:16), and their role in "telling" us about God is
fairly easy to see if we are not blinded by an insistence on the unprov-
able position that "there is no God" (Psalm 14:1).

What may often be overlooked in the "day unto day" routine
(Psalm 19:1-2) of our existence is that the very dependability of each
day's processes is a wonderful testimony to the design, purposes, and
faithfulness of the Creator. The whole core of evolutionary naturalism,
however, is randomness—an unknowable and undependable chaos
and disorder. The universe, on the other hand, is very stable!

- The sun always rises in the east and sets in the west.

- The earth always turns on its axis and cycles through its day
  at the same speed.

- The dependable clockwork precision of the tides always
  regulates much of our life.

- Seasons always come and go, planting and harvesting
  always follow each other dependably, and life is always
  conceived and born with regularity.

After the awful judgment of the great flood of Noah's day, God gave
a solemn promise to Noah, and through him to all living creatures.

With that promise, God placed in effect the same creative power that brought the universe into existence (Colossians 1:17), but He now focused His grace and mercy on keeping the universe stable until He finalizes His plans for eternity (2 Peter 3:7).

> The Lord said in his heart, I will not again curse the ground any more for man's sake; for the imagination of man's heart is evil from his youth; neither will I again smite any more every thing living, as I have done. While the earth remaineth, seedtime and harvest, and cold and heat, and summer and winter, and day and night shall not cease (Genesis 8:21-22).

This wordless language is easily read by all humanity and openly declares that God is awesomely omnipotent and omniscient as well as lovingly compassionate and faithful. All living creatures depend on this.

The night also teaches us about God.

Abundant evidence of God's wisdom and provision can be found within our own galaxy. Unlike many other galaxies, the Milky Way contains just the right balance of stars and planets needed to support life on earth. And our solar system is situated within the Milky Way so that it is far enough from the central region to escape the immense radiation from the stars concentrated there. The lower radiation in our vicinity also gives us a clearer window to observe and study the universe beyond our galaxy.

We live in a time when our knowledge of the heavens is expanding quickly. This knowledge should lead us to praise God for His amazing provision and protection. The cause of the laws of nature is not found in nature, but beyond nature. The heavens declare evidence for creation by their beauty, size, and order.

The heavens declare evidence for creation
by their beauty, size, and order.

Summarizing the Evidence

Nature is God's language for all humanity. The first law of thermodynamics says the universe couldn't be making itself, and the second law says it is running down. Thus, the universe had a beginning and a Beginner.

The earth is unique. Almost every observable characteristic of the planet is exactly fine-tuned for life, just as though it was intended to harbor life as God's Word clearly reveals.

The declaration of the heavens. The heavens are so energy-packed and so well-organized that they could have found their origins only in an infinitely powerful and infinitely wise Source.

Biblical Insight

Read Job 12:7-10.

1. What is meant by the command "Speak to the earth"?

2. What is the answer to the question in verse 9?

3. Which verses in Romans 1 most directly relate to this passage in Job?

4. Why do those who deny creation scoff so venomously in their denials? (Compare John 3:19.)

Evidence from Physical Science

*...that their hearts might be comforted, being knit together in love,
and unto all riches of the full assurance of understanding, to the
acknowledgement of the mystery of God, and of the Father, and of
Christ; in whom are hid all the treasures of wisdom and knowledge.*

Colossians 2:2-3

*This most beautiful system of the sun, planets, and
comets, could only proceed from the counsel and
dominion of an intelligent and powerful Being.*

Sir Isaac Newton

 Evidence for special creation surrounds us. Everywhere from microscopic elements to the unfathomable recesses of the universe, the Creator speaks to us through the things He has made.

Where does everything come from, and what does it mean? Science is limited in its ability to answer the questions nearest to our hearts. However, science does give us tools to understand our universe and the laws of nature that we can observe today. This understanding provides compelling evidence for creation.

Topsy-Turvy

Woe unto them that call evil good, and good evil; that put darkness for light, and light for darkness; that put bitter for sweet, and sweet for bitter! Woe unto them that are wise in their own eyes, and prudent in their own sight! (Isaiah 5:20-21).

The term *topsy-turvy* has been around since the sixteenth century. The various usages of it convey a sense of the confusion and chaos that one feels when things are not the way they are supposed to be. I remember hearing similar terms as a child: *higgledy-piggledy*, *hugger-mugger*, and *head over heels*.

The book *The Grand Design* by Stephen Hawking and Leonard Mlodinow is a prime example of such topsy-turvy thinking. The very title itself is higgledy-piggledy. The grand design it refers to is no design at all! Hawking and Mlodinow spend enormous intellectual capital to demonstrate that even though things seem to work beautifully in our universe, there is absolutely no reason to conclude that Someone or something (other than the universe itself) is responsible for what we observe.

Their position is that we cannot observe anything for sure. We are like a goldfish in a glass bowl. Our perspective is warped by the environment in which we live. If we could somehow get out of our bowl, we might be able to see differently. But for now, Hawking and Mlodinow conclude, God is not at all necessary to consider when we observe and think about the origin and maintenance of the universe. In fact, the goldfish's viewpoint of the universe is just as valid as our own.

The psalmist asked, "Why do the heathen rage, and the people imagine a vain thing?" (Psalm 2:1). Often we feel the weight of the godless pundits who spit their venom at the Creator who loved them and died for them. Surely we can expect such rebellion, and many times those who openly shake their intellectual fist at the King of kings seem to be "in great power, and spreading [themselves] like a green bay tree" (Psalm 37:35). They seem to have the resources, the logistics, and the overall advantage to promote their worldview of atheistic and evolutionary naturalism.

But I would have you remember two grand and unalterable facts. First, "the heavens declare the glory of God; and the firmament showeth his handiwork" (Psalm 19:1). Nothing will prevent the message of the Creator from reaching those whose hearts are open to the message. No raging by the heathens will ever mute the message of the "invisible things" of our Creator—so "they are without excuse" (Romans 1:20).

Yes, we are to be spokespersons and ambassadors for the gospel, but our witness is framed by the undeniable backdrop of the creation itself. That message goes out in surround sound—the sound of the glory of God and with the very power of God as we announce the good news!

Second, those who reject or resist the message will not win! "He that sitteth in the heavens shall laugh: the Lord shall have them in derision" (Psalm 2:4). The wickedness of our time in history may make us feel small and impotent, but we are saved "to the uttermost" (Hebrews 7:25), commissioned with the "unsearchable riches of Christ" (Ephesians 3:8), and guaranteed to be "conformed to the image of his Son" (Romans 8:29).

> For I am persuaded, that neither death, nor life, nor angels, nor principalities, nor powers, nor things present, nor things to come, nor height, nor depth, nor any other creature, shall be able to separate us from the love of God, which is in Christ Jesus our Lord (Romans 8:38-39).

The physical universe of space, time, and matter has not always existed, but was supernaturally created by a transcendent personal Creator who alone has existed from eternity. The laws of science demonstrate that mass and energy were created to last. Our place in the universe is perfectly balanced for life. Many branches of science study the laws of mass, energy, and the forces of nature at all levels of scale.

The Universe Demands a Designer

Everyone knows the universe looks designed.

Naturalists want to explain the universe as a necessary outcome of laws and initial conditions instead of a roll of the dice. The Big Bang theory, inflation, and the search for structure in the cosmic background radiation are all part of this tradition. The design argument took on renewed urgency in the 1930s when quantum physicists realized that certain constants, such as the force of gravity and the charge on the electron, could have taken arbitrary values, yet most values would never produce a universe with atoms, stars, planets, or observers.

One early escape from the design inference was the so-called anthropic principle, which basically states that the conditions that make intelligent life possible and intelligent life itself were inevitable, but most naturalists have dismissed such speculations as metaphysical fluff.

Some hoped that superstring theory would rescue the apparent purposeful design of the universe from its obvious implications to a Creator, but its champions found that their equations permit 10^{500} different sets of initial conditions—most of them life-prohibiting.

The only way our universe could be explained, therefore, was either by a Designer who chose the right values or by luck among untold numbers of alternate universes with random values.

One of the basic axioms in science is the principle of Occam's razor. In its simplest form, Occam's razor states that one should make no more assumptions than are needed. That "keep it simple" principle would surely prefer a single Designer to uncountable universes.

The universe displays unimaginable power.

Beyond the power that lights the universe with stars is our Creator, who carefully balances the laws of nature. A star is a continuous explosion of awesome power. The power to create a universe with billions of galaxies, each with billions of stars, is beyond imagination. Only a Creator who is outside of nature can create mass and energy.

The universe displays exquisite order.

The laws of nature point to a power greater than themselves. These laws are balanced so that our sun provides us with energy day by day and so that the molecules within us can use that energy.

Light from stars and the sun begins with hydrogen. Hydrogen is the most plentiful element in the universe. The sun is a large ball of very hot hydrogen. It is more than 100 times as wide as the earth. The energy of the sun comes from nuclear explosions of hydrogen. These are much more powerful than chemical explosions.

Gravity draws all the sun's hydrogen together, creating intense pressure. In the core of the sun, the huge forces cause nuclear fusion reactions. Hydrogen atoms fuse together into helium and release huge amounts of energy.

These explosions do not cause the sun to suddenly blow up and then go cold. The balanced laws of physics hold our sun together. Gravity pulls the atoms back as each explosion pushes them away. This balance keeps the billions of stars in billions of galaxies burning.

The universe displays absolute precision.

If the laws of nature were just slightly different, the delicate balance would not exist between hydrogen, oxygen, and carbon. Without this balance, thousands of critical molecular interactions would not happen. Only a few elements have the unique properties to sustain life. Any change would make life impossible.

The universe is only several thousand years old. Comets are an example of a natural clock within our solar system. With each orbit around the sun, comets lose considerable mass. They cannot be very old because they cannot survive many orbits.

To get around this problem, many astronomers assume there is a vast cloud of comets near the edge of the solar system, and new comets are released every so often. This imaginary cloud is called the Oort cloud, named after the astronomer who proposed it. The problem is that there is no observational evidence that such a cloud exists at all.

Each year our knowledge of astronomy increases with new evidence concerning the origin of our solar system, our galaxy, and our universe. We can make assumptions beyond what can be observed and verified, but the heavens continue to bear witness to recent creation.

FANTASTIC FLYBY OF COMET HARTLEY 2

In late 2010, NASA's Deep Impact spacecraft photographed a quirky comet, roughly one mile long and shaped like a dumbbell, named Hartley 2. The comet orbits the sun every 6.46 years, so it should return to earth's neighborhood in 2017. It loses an outer layer of its icy material from the erosive force of solar wind each time it nears the sun. Like most comets, Hartley 2 is getting smaller.

But it has not yet completely eroded, so it cannot be older than thousands of years. Comets have never been seen entering the solar system, and no extrasolar stash of comets is known, so comets must have formed at the same time as the solar system. But their youthfulness refutes the solar system's 4.6 billion-year age assignment.

Even more strangely, one end of Hartley 2 is vigorously outgassing carbon dioxide, and the NASA images show it ejecting chunks of ice out into space. This means that Hartley 2 must be even younger! At current rates, Hartley 2 will spend all of itself in about 700 years.[1]

Evolutionary astronomers have no idea where the explosive pressure is coming from or why or how it retains a supply of carbon dioxide gas. However, none of these observations surprise biblical astronomers.

The Universe Is Stable

The universe was created sometime in the past and has been decreasing in available energy ever since. The light from distant galaxies confirms that chemical elements behave in the same way there as they do here on earth.

Energy cannot be created or destroyed.

One of the most basic laws of science is the law of the conservation of energy. Energy cannot be created or destroyed; it can only be changed from one form to another.

Energy is not currently being created. The universe could not have created itself using natural processes because nature did not exist before the universe came into existence. Something beyond nature must have created all the energy and matter we see today. Present measures of energy are enormous beyond understanding, indicating a power source so great that *infinite* is the best word we have to describe it.

The logical conclusion is that a supernatural Creator with infinite power created the universe. There is no other energy source capable of originating what we observe today.

> The logical conclusion is that a supernatural Creator
> with infinite power created the universe.

Available energy decreases over time.

There is less available energy today than there was yesterday. The second law of thermodynamics states that the entropy of an isolated system that is not in equilibrium, such as the universe, will tend to increase over time, approaching a maximum value at equilibrium. *Entropy* refers to the loss of organization that constantly occurs in matter and the various forms of energy. The third law of thermodynamics states that as the temperature approaches absolute zero, the entropy of a system approaches a constant.

Fortunately for us, the temperature of the universe is not absolute zero. It is moving that way each moment, but it is not there yet.

At some prior time, all the energy in the universe was available. Energy must have been created at some finite time in the past; otherwise we would have died long ago. The logical conclusion is that an infinite Creator made the universe a finite time ago.

Elements are dependable across the universe.

The visible energy from the sun is the sunshine that lights the day and the light reflected by the moon at night. The range of colors visible in a rainbow is actually a very small part of the electromagnetic spectrum.

Chemicals give off and absorb light at specific points on the electromagnetic spectrum. By comparing the light from various chemicals with the light from our sun, we have learned that our sun is made up mostly of hydrogen. We have also learned which atoms are in galaxies far away. The chemical elements across the universe behave the same way they do on earth.

Processes today operate primarily within fixed natural laws and relatively uniform process rates, but these laws were themselves originally created and are daily maintained by their Creator, so there is always the possibility of miraculous intervention in these laws or processes by their Creator.

The earth was uniquely created.

If left to chance, the universe probably couldn't support life anywhere. God created our planet for life to thrive. As we learn how special our planet is within the entire universe, we learn of our Creator's faithfulness to us.

Our sun has been placed at the perfect location within our galaxy, and our planet has been placed at the perfect location within our solar system. Our planet was created to protect the life that God placed here. Even the atmosphere and oceans of our planet have been carefully designed to provide the right amount of energy and fresh water.

Our solar system is perfectly located within our galaxy.

The spiral-shaped galaxy in which the earth is located is called the Milky Way. The spiraling arms and center of this galaxy contain many stars set close together, giving off its characteristic brightness.

Other galaxies—older, smaller, elliptical, and irregular—are missing the proper amounts of elements necessary to maintain the right balance of stars and planets required to support life.

Some stars explode into supernovas, causing deadly radiation to flow through nearby stars and planets.

The center and arms of galaxies are flooded with high amounts of radiation. Most stars are located in places with too much harmful energy for life. Moreover, at that location we could not observe farther than a few light-years into the rest of the universe because the nearby stars would completely block our view.

Our solar system is located about two-thirds of the way out toward the edge of the Milky Way, where we are least likely to suffer collisions with other stars. Most of the stars in our galaxy are within the larger spiral arms or in the center. Because there are few stars near us, there is a low amount of radiation surrounding our solar system. And we can observe the rest of the universe and our own galaxy much better as a result.

Our planet is perfectly located within our solar system.

The earth appears to be near the center of the universe. Galaxies look the same and are moving away from us in all directions. The cosmic microwave background radiation comes to us very uniformly from all directions. These and other data strongly indicate we are located at a very special location by design.

Instead of accepting the obvious, recent models of physical cosmology assume that the earth is not special and that objects would appear to be receding the same way from any other spot in the universe. Instead of measuring the age of the universe in thousands of years, this assumption measures it in billions of years.

In contrast, creation cosmologies explain the data by starting from biblically based axioms: The cosmos has a unique center and a boundary for its matter, beyond which there is at least some empty space. On a cosmic scale of distances, the earth is near the center.

Our solar system also contains thousands of asteroids and meteoroids. These sometimes collide with planets. Jupiter keeps many large rocks from hitting earth by attracting them with its strong gravity.

The earth's huge moon also protects us from many of the rocks that cross our planet's path. The craters across the moon's surface demonstrate that many objects have collided with the moon instead of earth. The moon's South Pole–Aitken basin is the largest known crater in our solar system. It is 8 miles deep and 1500 miles across. The earth's moon is unusually large.

In addition, our huge moon is a stabilizing anchor for our planet. It prevents our planet from tilting too far from the attraction of the sun or Jupiter.

We are protected by the design of our solar system.

Our planet was created for life.

Our solar system is filled with amazing planets, but none are perfect for life except the earth.

Mercury is the closest planet to the sun. It has a very slow spin, so it gets very hot and very cold. The side facing the sun is heated to 800 degrees Fahrenheit, and the side away from the sun is cooled to -298 degrees Fahrenheit.

> Our solar system is filled with amazing planets,
> but none are perfect for life except the earth.

Venus is even hotter than Mercury yet farther away from the sun. Venus has an atmosphere 90 times thicker than earth's. Heat is trapped in the clouds and heats the entire planet to 931 degrees Fahrenheit.

Mars is similar to earth in many ways. A day on Mars is 24.7 hours. It is tilted 25 degrees, just two more degrees than earth. At its warmest, it can get to be a comfortable 67 degrees Fahrenheit. It has two small moons. But Mars is smaller than earth, so its gravity is only a third of earth's. Without enough gravity, Mars is unable to hold a larger atmosphere. What atmosphere it has is made of gases we cannot breathe. Without much of an atmosphere, many meteoroids hit Mars. It also gets very cold at night.

Jupiter is the largest planet in our solar system. It is ten times smaller than the sun and ten times larger than the earth. Jupiter spins faster than any other planet, with a day of 9 hours and 55.5 minutes. Its fast spin causes tremendous storms. The big red spot on Jupiter is actually a huge hurricane.

Saturn is the second-largest planet in our solar system and has the largest set of rings. It is almost twice as far away from the sun as Jupiter. Saturn is a gas giant. As one descends into the atmosphere, the pressure, temperature, and gravity greatly increase. The core of the planet is boiling hot and radiates more heat out into space than it receives from the sun.

Uranus is tilted on its side with its axis pointed at the sun. If the earth's axis was pointed at the sun, one hemisphere would always be boiling hot and the other would be freezing cold. Uranus is four times as far from the sun as Jupiter and twice as far from the sun as Saturn.

Neptune is the farthest gas giant from the sun. It is almost four times larger than the earth. Its strong gravity traps harmful gases in its atmosphere.

Each planet in our solar system demonstrates that earth is unique and specially created for life. Similarly, among the hundreds of extra-solar planets that have been recently discovered, none have even the most fundamental life-support properties.

A smaller planet, such as Mars, would be unable to hold our atmosphere, which protects us from meteoroids and keeps the temperature within the range needed for life.

A larger planet, like Neptune, would trap too much atmosphere. The pressure and temperature would greatly increase. A stronger gravity from the increased size would also trap harmful gases in the atmosphere.

Earth has a strong magnetic field. This protects us from harmful radiation from the sun.

Our water cycle protects us and provides for us.

Clouds function as curtains for the earth, balancing the temperature. They block the sun when the temperature on earth becomes too hot and let the sunlight in when it becomes too cold. When the earth is hot, more water evaporates from the oceans and turns into clouds. These clouds reflect more energy, and the earth cools. When the earth is cold, the clouds cool and condense into rain and snow. With fewer clouds, less energy is reflected. The energy reaches the earth and warms it. The earth has the most diverse collection of reflective surfaces in our solar system.

Water is the most abundant chemical compound on earth. Water covers three-fourths of the earth's surface. Your body is one-half to three-fourths water. Water is ideal for carbon-based biochemistry.

Water is transported from oceans to the atmosphere, to the land, and then back to the oceans. Oceans are the primary storehouses of water on the earth. The sun evaporates water from the oceans, the evaporated water then rises into the atmosphere, and eventually it returns to the ocean.

The atmosphere also stores a small quantity of water. Cooling water vapor condenses into clouds. Water falls back to the land as rain and snow.

The land also stores water. Fresh water is held for months and years in the form of ice and snow. Water infiltrates the land and is stored underground. Surface water flows into streams and river. Lakes store water. Water flows from the land back into the ocean.

Water expands when it freezes, unlike most other substances. Ice and snow take up more volume than the same amount of liquid water. This makes water denser as a liquid than when it is frozen, so ice floats on the surface. If ice did not float on the surface of the water, the floors of oceans and lakes would be covered with glaciers of ice that never melted. Ice helps regulate the climate by reflecting energy.

Water's temperature range is perfect for cycling water from the oceans to the land. Water takes a lot of energy to evaporate into a vapor, and it releases this energy when it condenses back into liquid. This absorption and release of energy balances temperatures in the earth's climate and inside living cells. If less energy were required for evaporation, streams, rivers, and lakes would evaporate away quickly.

Summarizing the Evidence

- The first and second laws of thermodynamics prove that the universe had a beginning.

- The host of specifications for life found in the solar system and on earth can only have found their origins in a Creator such as described in Scripture.

Biblical Insight

Psalm 104 is often considered a creation psalm. Consider as you investigate the psalm:

1. Does the psalmist distinguish between the power required to sustain creation and all its operations from that required to have created it in the beginning?

2. Considering the climactic verse 24, what are some specific features of God's creation that reveal His wisdom and yet are not mentioned in Psalm 104?

3. List three verbs describing how one should react to or interact with God in view of His illustrated attributes.

5

Evidence from Earth Science

*Bless the LORD, O my soul. O LORD my God, thou art very
great; thou art clothed with honor and majesty… Who laid the
foundations of the earth, that it should not be removed for ever.*

Psalm 104:1,5

*A circular argument arises: Interpret the fossil record in the terms
of a particular theory of evolution, inspect the interpretation, and
note that it confirms the theory. Well, it would, wouldn't it?*

Tom Kemp

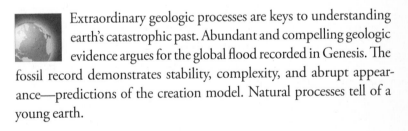 Extraordinary geologic processes are keys to understanding earth's catastrophic past. Abundant and compelling geologic evidence argues for the global flood recorded in Genesis. The fossil record demonstrates stability, complexity, and abrupt appearance—predictions of the creation model. Natural processes tell of a young earth.

The global flood is the key to the past.

Widespread marine strata and fossils in the earth's highest mountains and on elevated continental plateaus imply that the ocean once covered the continents. Large geologic structures that formed quickly provide worldwide evidence of a global flood. Sedimentary rock beds that were rapidly formed cover the earth. A big, water-based event happened in the recent past to form the geologic features we see around us.

The issue of whether the worldwide flood of Noah's day took place as described in the Bible makes an enormous difference in how a geologist or paleontologist looks at the data entombed in the rocks of the earth.

To begin with, the rock strata and fossil remains are the only empirical clues that scientists have about the ancient past of earth's history. If indeed the strata were laid down over millions of years, no human was alive to record the events. If, however, the strata were deposited by a global deluge as presented by the information in the Bible, all who are alive today are dependent on the eyewitness account of that flood.

Science cannot reproduce the geologic processes. The best a scientist can do with the unobserved past is to evaluate the clues in the rocks and the fossils and try to understand them in the light of present processes or by studying much smaller hydraulic forces.

Historical science is framed by the scientist's presuppositions, or belief system. If the scientist embraces the naturalistic and evolutionary point of view, he will interpret the data in the light of that view. The same is true for a scientist who embraces the biblical point of view. The two scientists would look at the same data and come to very different conclusions.

If the biblical account of a global flood is true, as the Bible teaches, then most of the rock strata and nearly all of the fossil remains were laid down during one year. If the evolutionary view is true, then the bias of present uniformitarian conditions will lead to the conclusion that the time lapse is millions of years.

All science makes predictions based on hypotheses. This is especially true of historical science because the scientist was not around to see the actual event take place. The hypothesis that finds the most predictions to be in agreement with the facts is most likely to be correct. When predictions about a model or theory are not corroborated by the data, science suggests that the hypothesis is not correct.

Testing the validity of predictions is an important method to verify the accuracy of a theory.

Much evidence exists for a worldwide flood.

History is not open to direct scientific testing. Geologists, therefore, interpret the geologic record using their limited understanding of modern geologic processes, typically by comparing the record with slow processes known to occur in history.

Twentieth-century geologists taught the familiar maximum "The present is the key to the past." However, geologists in the past 30 years have recognized evidence supporting regional, continental, and global catastrophic events that appear to have formed the major portion of the strata. Natural disasters and their aftermaths have direct application to interpreting the geologic record.

> Twentieth-century geologists taught the familiar maximum "The present is the key to the past."

Catastrophist patterns of interpretation have thoroughly permeated conventional thinking about the geologic record. Geologists are deliberately reevaluating outdated uniformitarian thinking and are increasingly adopting a global catastrophic model. Now that catastrophic processes are widely employed to describe the strata record, twenty-first-century geologists are wondering whether natural disasters are the key to the past.

Strata and the marine fossils they contain provide critical evidence that the oceans once covered the continents, even the highest continental areas. Extremely widespread strata deposits, or *sequences*, argue for an intercontinental or global flood.

Water deposited the sediments comprising what is called the Sauk sequence, so that means water covered North America and some of Europe at that time. Muddy water also covered much of North America and perhaps some of Europe and Africa when it deposited the Tippecanoe sequence of sedimentary rock layers. Some red-colored sedimentary rock layers called *redbeds* span across continents, as do certain volcanic layers called *tuff beds* and even some coal layers.

Experiments and observations have proven that grains of sediment carried by fast-moving water cause very rapid stratification, or layering. Certain mudflows produced sequences of broad, flat rocks called *plane beds*. They also formed thick *graded beds*, where the grain sizes are larger near the bottom and very small at the top. These appear to have been sorted by a single event, yet they are dozens of feet thick.

And when fast-flowing water moved in one direction for a long time, it produced crisscrossing layers of sediment called *cross beds*. Revealing flume studies recreated these conditions, showing that water rapidly built cross beds by sweeping grains from underwater dunes and piling them in layers on lee side of the dunes. Some of these flows were so unimaginably powerful that they formed underwater dunes dozens of feet thick, resulting in giant sandstone formations called *hummocky beds*, or *hummocky cross-stratification*.

All young-earth and most old-earth advocates agree that the layers themselves represent short periods of time. Thus, the length of time indicated by the contact between those layers, when erosion and not deposition would have dominated, will give us the approximate time required for the entire set of visible sedimentary rock layers. This draws our attention to the upper surface of each layer. Is there evidence—such as erosion ruts, cuts and rills, or color changes from long exposure to oxygen in the atmosphere—that they laid exposed for great ages? If instead the contacts are flat and smooth, this would indicate that each layer covered the one below it too quickly for erosion or atmospheric chemistry to have occurred.

If each rock layer took a short time to form and there's no trace of time in between them, then all the rock layers took a short time to form, as if a great flood made them. These and many other obvious evidences are leading many geologists to construct a global flood model for earth history.

Geologic processes were catastrophic.

Earth's geologic strata have been characterized by evolutionists as representing millions of years of accumulation of sediments under water. Modern observers are generally willing to recognize evidence of rapid deposition of the strata by catastrophic processes, but they insist that long spans of time passed between depositional episodes. During these long ages, erosion may have occurred, but they say the whole package required great ages.

Creationists, on the other hand, consider that the bulk of earth's sedimentary rock accumulated rapidly beneath the waters of the great flood of Noah's day. One layer followed another in swift succession, sometimes interrupted by brief periods of quiet, uplift, and erosion. Some time may have passed between depositional events, but these periods were not long, and the bulk of the sedimentary rock record may represent hardly more than one year.

Regional, continental, and global catastrophic processes are so prominent in the geologic record that many geologists are reorganizing their thinking to better discern and understand these extraordinary events.

Like sand on a seashore, many layers exhibit ripple marks. Yet ripple marks in loose sand last only until the next tide. Even in hard rock they erode within a few years. Their nearly ubiquitous presence on sandstone surfaces argues for quick burial, perhaps by the next wave, protecting them until they hardened.

A similar line of reasoning notes that animal burrows, plant roots, and the like can be found on every modern soil surface, on land or in water. Why are they rare to nonexistent in the geologic record? Sometimes a fossil tree or animal body will intersect more than one layer. Called *polystrate* fossils, they demand a short time between layer depositions.

An erosional surface in the rocks is called an *unconformity*, and some amount of time is necessary between two unconformable layers. But unconformities are not found worldwide. When followed for long lateral stretches, they often grade into one another, implying continual (rapid) deposition of each layer in the whole sequence of layers. On a larger scale, entire geologic periods, such as the Cambrian or Ordovician, are present, implying a short duration. Sometimes they grade conformably into the next period.

From the Cambrian period upward, the geologic strata are a record of continuous, catastrophic, rapid deposition under flood waters. This is what we would expect based on the biblical account of the great flood.

Geologic evidence indicates rapid formation.

There is extensive evidence that the layers of strata in the geologic record were laid down very quickly, similar to the processes observed when Mount Saint Helens erupted. Rapid global formation of sedimentary rock beds is evidence that the age of the earth is thousands of years, not millions.

The major formations of the earth's crust are sedimentary rock beds. These were formed by rapid erosion, transportation, and deposition by water. There is no global evidence of great lengths of time between these layers or indications that these layers took long periods of time to form.

For example, a layer of Tapeats sandstone is a major feature of the lower part of the Grand Canyon. The same rock layer, with different local names, is found in Utah, Wyoming, Montana, Colorado, South Dakota, the Midwest, the Ozarks, and northern New York State. Equivalent formations are found across wide portions of Canada, eastern Greenland, and Scotland.

Skeptics of creation science often claim that no evidence for the flood exists. Even though most geologists have abandoned old-style uniformity and grudgingly accepted major catastrophism, they still deny the global yearlong cataclysm of Noah's day described in Scripture.

Obviously, we can't observe that past event, but if such a world-restructuring flood occurred, what would we expect to result from it?

When considering nonrepeatable events, we are limited to scientific predictions—not predictions of the future, but predictions of the evidence. Reasoning from the biblical record, we would predict that when we examine the geologic results of the flood, we will see that the geologic strata were deposited by catastrophic processes operating on a regional scale. These large-scale results would dominate the rock record. Uniformitarian scientists would predict that the record would be dominated by the slow and gradual geologic processes observed today, operating on a local scale. Once both sides have made their predictions, the evidence can be evaluated as to which one is the better fit. That one is more likely correct.

Consider the Columbia River Basalt Group of lava flows in Washington, Oregon, and Idaho. This series of lava flows was stacked one on top of another in rapid succession and covers an area of some 65,000 square miles, with a volume of about 40,000 cubic miles. This dwarfs the largest historic lava flow, which occurred in Iceland in 1783 and covered an area of about 200 square miles, with a volume of less than 3 cubic miles. One can scarcely envision such eruptions, which produced a veritable lake of lava thousands of times larger than anything we have seen in the modern era. The molten material flowed from several locations along cracks in the earth's surface. But even this deposit is dwarfed by other much larger basalt deposits that have been recognized.

Occurring in layers stratigraphically below the Columbia River Basalts are thick layers of water-deposited, fossil-bearing, sedimentary rock, obviously deposited by the flood itself. Thus, flood advocates interpret these megaeruptions of basalt as probably occurring during the very last stages of the flood or in the years of readjustment that followed as earth's systems regained the relative equilibrium we see now. Surely this was a fearful time.

Obviously such large-scale volcanism does not match uniformitarian predictions regarding the past. Yet it does match the creation/flood/young-earth prediction of catastrophic processes operating on a regional scale during and immediately following the flood. Neither side can directly observe the past, but the biblical model is the one that best predicts the evidence and is thus, from a scientific perspective, more likely correct.

Worldwide catastrophic evidence is everywhere.

Tremendous amounts of water moving very quickly have left scars throughout the earth's major formations. Catastrophic displacements of enormous plates of the earth's crust most probably provided the driving force for the global flood and definitely produced the deep spaces for the water to drain into afterward.

The majority of our planet's sedimentary rock appears to have accumulated rapidly by means of a worldwide deluge. Single layers quickly covered large parts of the globe. Some of the rock surfaces that are right next to a fault contain tiny broken pieces of rock that were cemented together, called *microbreccias*. Other rocks near ancient faults are called *pseudotachylites* because they look like smooth, glassy volcanic rocks but their surfaces were actually wiped with tremendous friction. These show rapid and unprecedentedly powerful earth movements.

Broad, beveled surfaces below and within thick strata provide evidence of widespread, rapid sediment-building during a global flood. For example, the contact between the Coconino sandstone and Hermit shale as seen on the Bright Angel Trail in the Grand Canyon shows no sign of eons of erosion. Instead, it is just as flat, sharp, and broad as the contacts between the other major Grand Canyon rock layers. However, elsewhere in Arizona, 2000 feet of sedimentary strata are found between these same two sandstone and shale layers. No natural process could have lifted the Coconino sandstone off the top of the Hermit shale in certain areas in Arizona, deposited thousands of feet of water-borne sediment on the Hermit shale, and then set the Coconino back down like a continental sandwich—all without breaking the Coconino or leaving traces of erosion. Therefore, all these layers must have been deposited at around the same time—during the yearlong Genesis flood.

> As further evidence for the worldwide nature of the flood, ancient human cultures across the globe appear to possess legends recounting a great global flood.

Rules of Evidence and the Fossil Record

Over the past centuries, the search for truth in science has been formalized into the process known as the scientific method. Theories are developed and tested according to a generally accepted standard. In a similar fashion, the legal profession operates by what is known as the rules of evidence. In legal controversies, the rules of evidence serve as a vital vehicle for seriously searching out and reliably reaching the truth. Real truth stands up to being tested. And even the absence of evidence can operate as a silent witness, testifying to a circumstance where there is nothing when there should be something.

In a Medicare fraud case involving years of federal court proceedings, one of the appeals was finally decided in 2007. Part of the convicting evidence was nothing—literally nothing—when there should have been something.

From a circumstantial evidence standpoint, the government's proof of "nothing" (in this case, missing verification of the fraudulent doctor's treatment of patients) clearly demonstrated that the doctor had not provided evidence that he had indeed cared for the people for whom he had billed the Medicare system.

This illustrates the power of an argument from silence. The forensic force of such a silent witness can buttress a sentence of felony jail time. But how can "nothing" become admissible circumstantial evidence at trial? Federal evidence rule 803(10) provides one such forensic possibility. Essentially, the absence of a record, or the nonoccurrence or nonexistence of a matter that would normally have been recorded, can serve as evidence in its own right, provided that a sufficiently diligent search failed to disclose the record.

Evidence rule 803(7) is similar, but it applies to records that have a relevant "absence" of an entry, as well as where and when a documentary "nothing" is forensically important.

What would happen if we applied the same principles of the evidence rules to analyzing the scientific controversies about origins? How does the evidence of nothing demonstrated by this particular Medicare fraud scheme relate to the question of origins? The comparison can be illustrated by applying the evidence rules that govern "nothing when there should be something" to the problem of missing links. This evidentiary insight may be unusual, but it is certainly not new.

When examining the quest for missing links, the evidence is not there—there is literally nothing when there should have been something. To use the logic of rule 803(10), a diligent search for these so-called transitional form fossils over a period of 150 years has failed to disclose them. These years of diligent search indicate a glaring absence of molecules-to-man evolutionary phylogeny (history of development) in the fossil record. In other words, the empirical data of earth's fossils, if analyzed forensically, show that evolutionary development is just empty imaginings, refuted by the evidence of nothing.

Evolutionists often speak of missing links. They say that the bridge between man and the apes is the missing link, the hypothetical apelike ancestor of both. But missing links should appear all over the evolutionary tree. For instance, dogs and bears are thought to be evolutionary cousins, related to each other through a missing link. The same could be said for every other branch on the tree. All of the animal types are thought to have arisen by the transformation of some other animal type, and at each branching node is a missing link, and between the node and the modern form are many more. If you still don't know what a missing link is, don't worry. No one knows what a missing link is because they are missing! We've never seen one.

This argument from silence is an absence in the evidentiary record—a "nothing where there should be something" if evolutionary theory were true. But evolutionary theory is not true, so the real world's fossil record has been providing irrefutable evidence—by the absence of missing links—for a long, long time.

Some may say that the above analysis is much ado about nothing. However, so much false science is involved in support of evolution, we must use the greatest care and the highest standards in our quest to uncover the true history of our world. And sometimes, "nothing" is itself evidence for the truth.

Fossils show stasis and not transitional forms.

The fossil record demonstrates abrupt appearance, complexity at all stratigraphic levels, and maintenance of defining characteristics (or stasis). These primary features of the fossil record are predictions of the creation model.

Evolution models for the fossil record require three main predictions:

- wholesale change of organisms through time
- primitive organisms giving rise to complex organisms
- gradual derivation of new organisms producing transitional forms

Obviously, these two positions and their predictions are opposites and cannot be merged into some sort of hybrid theory. A careful scientist would use these predictions to evaluate the available evidence to determine which model is the most correct.

Fossils show the immediate appearance of complex life.

The fossil record reflects the original diversity of life, not an evolving tree of increasing complexity. When a fossil appears in the sedimentary rock layers, it appears in a fully developed form with no undisputed evidence for a transitional ancestor at all.

Trilobites, extinct but well-designed arthropods that lived on the ocean bottom, appear suddenly in the fossil record without any transitions. There are no intermediate fossils between simple single-cell organisms, such as bacteria, and complex invertebrates, such as trilobites. Extinct trilobites had as much organized complexity as any of today's invertebrates. In addition to trilobites, billions of other fossils have been found that suddenly appear fully formed, such as clams, snails, sponges, and jellyfish. More than 300 different body plans are found without any fossil transitions between them and single-cell organisms.

Fish have no ancestors or transitional forms that show how invertebrates, many with their skeletons on the outside, could have become vertebrates with internal skeletons.

Fossils of a wide variety of flying and crawling insects appear without any transitions. Dragonflies, for example, appear suddenly in the fossil record. The highly complex systems that enable the dragonfly's aerodynamic abilities have no precedents in the fossil record.

Evolutionists sometimes claim that they have abundant evidence of transitions, but when pressed, the examples are almost always minor variations within a category that fall within the normal variation expected in living kinds. They are certainly not proof of evolution.

In general, evolutionists are quick to admit the almost complete lack of transitional fossils. In fact, many of the current leaders in evolutionary thought have made their careers attempting to explain this lack by proposing that evolution of isolated groups occurred so rapidly in the past that no individuals of the in-between forms were fossilized. Why should we expect to find fossils of organisms that existed only for a short time? Furthermore, they point out that fossilization rarely occurs today. It usually takes massive flooding and rapid burial.

Many believe that living creatures endured for vast time spans with stable body forms. These creatures were supposedly fossilized while in this equilibrium of stability. These long time spans were supposedly punctuated by short moments when creatures radically evolved. Conveniently, the evolutionary changes happened so fast that they were not recorded in the fossils. This story is called *punctuated equilibrium*. However, proponents of this idea have no biological explanation for how such rapid evolutionary leaps between basic kinds could have taken place. In the end, they are left with the same situation as those who believe in slow, gradual evolution—no evidence.

In the entire fossil record, there is not a single unequivocal transitional form proving a causal relationship between any two species. The billions of fossils we have discovered should include thousands of clear examples if they existed. This lack of transitions between species in the fossil record is what would be expected if life was created.

> In the entire fossil record, there is not a single unequivocal transitional form proving a causal relationship between any two species.

Fossils show rapid and catastrophic burial.

Fossils universally provide evidence of rapid burial and sometimes even agonizing death. Beveled surfaces below, within, and above thick strata sequences provide evidence of rapid erosion during and after the flood. Rapid burial is necessary to entomb organisms as the first step in fossilization. The abundant marine invertebrate fossils throughout the entire fossil strata demonstrate extraordinary burial conditions.

Very few fossils are forming today, and then only in the case of rapid burial by water. For instance, what happens to a fish when it dies? It either floats to the surface or sinks to the bottom, where it decays and is eaten by scavengers. Yet many fish fossils are so exquisitely preserved that even scales and organs are retained. Obviously there was no time for decay and bacterial action. We can certainly say something extraordinary happened to form the fossils. Furthermore, most fossils occur in huge fossil graveyards, where things from different habitats are mixed together in a watery grave. The predominant type of fossil is that of marine invertebrates, but these are found on the continents within catastrophically deposited rock units.

Each of the several different kinds of fossils requires rapid burial and circumstances that are seldom if ever at work today.

Polystrate fossil logs (tree trunks in vertical positions running through several sedimentary layers) are clear evidence of rapid burial. The term *polystrate* was coined to describe a fossil that is encased within more than one (*poly*) layer of rock (*strata*). These fossils tell a wonderful story that invalidates the commonly held uniformitarian idea of the slow and gradual accumulation of sediments.

These many-layered fossils are the exception to the rule, but they are known to all geologists. Trees are frequently found protruding out of coal seams into the strata above, and they sometimes extend into a second coal seam several feet above the first. Such fossils (or their remaining impressions) are found in many coal mines. There are also thin, reedlike stems extending through numerous layers. Furthermore, there are hundreds of individual fossils whose body widths exceed the width of the layers in which they are encased.

Obviously, the layers cannot be the result of slow accumulations. A dead fish, for example, will not remain whole for several years while sediment accumulates around it! No, it must be quickly buried in order to be preserved at all. Some of the big polystrate trees extend beyond strata otherwise thought to have required tens of thousands of years. Obviously, the entire section required less time than it takes a tree to rot and fall over.

It has now been well demonstrated that rapidly moving, sediment-laden fluids can result in an abundance of laminations and/or layers. They can be formed in lab experiments or by hurricanes. Some were even formed by catastrophic mud flows associated with the eruption of Mount Saint Helens.

Common vertebrate fossils also show rigor mortis and postures indicative of asphyxiation. (This was the case with archaeopteryx and dinosaur fossils in the quarry at Dinosaur National Monument.) This is hardly consistent with an evolutionary explanation of the fossil record.

Fossils are found at all upper levels.

The layers of sedimentary rock that cover the earth's surface contain marine creatures at all levels that appear suddenly and fully formed. The earth is covered with layers of sedimentary rock, formed from the sediment deposited by enormous water and mud flows. Those layers, which cover continents and are deposited by water, contain countless fossils.

As it turns out, 95 percent of all fossils are shallow marine invertebrates, mostly shellfish. For instance, clams are found in every layer. There are many different varieties of clams, but clams are in every layer and resemble the clams that are still alive today. There are no signs of evolution, just clams! The same is true of corals, jellyfish, and many other organisms. The fossil record documents primarily marine organisms buried in marine sediments, which (as we have seen) were catastrophically deposited.

Of the 5 percent of the remaining fossils, 95 percent of these are algae and plant fossils (4.75 percent of the total). In the remaining 5 percent of the 5 percent, insects and all other invertebrates make up 95 percent (0.2375 percent of the total).

All of the vertebrate fossils considered together (fish, amphibians, reptiles, birds, and mammals), comprise only 0.0125 percent of the entire fossil record, and only 1 percent of these, or 0.000125 percent of the total, consist of more than a single bone! Almost all of them come from the Ice Age. Surely, the vertebrate fossil record is far from complete.

When we look at the invertebrates, we see separate and distinct categories (clams, corals, trilobites, and so on) existing in the earliest strata with no hint of ancestors or of intermediates. We find clams by the trillions, with a lot of variety among them, but no evolution. Furthermore, we have no idea how vertebrate fish could have arisen from any invertebrate. Where good data are available, we see no evolution. Where the data are scanty, evolutionists create a story. The fossil record is volumi-nous and apparently substantially complete. Yet no evolution is seen.

> Where good data are available, we see no evolution.
> Where the data are scanty, evolutionists create a story.

The entire record of visible fossils consists mainly of marine inver-tebrates (animals without a backbone), including clams, jellyfish, and coral. But these ocean creatures are found primarily on the continents and rarely in the deep ocean basins. More clam shells are found on mountain peaks than under the ocean floor.

From the bottom layers to the top layers, most fossils are marine creatures. The upper levels do have an increasing number of vertebrates, such as fish, amphibians, reptiles, and mammals, but the fossils at the bottom levels are equally as complex as any animal today. All fossil types appear suddenly, fully formed and fully functional, without less complex ancestors under them.

The fossil record is strong evidence for the sudden appearance of life by creation, followed by rapid burial during a global flood.

Earth "Clocks"

How long is a billion years? The United States was founded a lit-tle more than 200 years ago. Columbus discovered the Americas more than 500 years ago. These events seem long ago, but the numbers are comparatively small. Continuing back in history, dates are less precise, but the pyramids in Egypt were built about 4000 years ago. The Asian empires were founded around the same time.

All of these events are rightly relegated to ancient history. Archae-ological artifacts and structures give only nebulous insights into the times of their origin. But in each of these cases we have at least some written history to aid us, scanty though it may be. For times older than these, the only reliable source we have is the biblical record. According to it, no civilization or record other than itself could exist before the great flood of Noah's day. Indeed, many ancient legends (of post-flood memories of pre-flood events) are fraught with illogic and mythology.

The Bible even places the creation of all things less than 2000 years before the flood. Our minds struggle with the antiquity implied in these thousands of years.

But can we comprehend one billion years? One billion seconds is approximately 32 years. One billion minutes takes us to the time of Christ. One billion hours is about 115,000 years—beyond any true comprehension. One billion days is nearly three million years. Think about it. What could one billion days possibly mean to an old man who has lived just 30,000 days?

One billion years cannot be grasped; neither can 4.67 billion years for the supposed age of the earth or 14 billion years or so since the so-called Big Bang. Tales of billions and billions of years are nothing more than arm-waving, perhaps capable of impressing or intimating but not of communicating understandable information.

A billion years might just as well be eternity, an equally unfathomable time-related word. Eternity future we can't comprehend either, but we believe it because the Creator of time promised it to us.

Measuring the rate at which natural processes function can provide a "clock" by which the world's outer age limit may be calculated. Many of these processes yield thousands of years rather than billions. In each case, assumptions must be applied.

The earth's magnetic field is decaying too fast.

The total energy stored in the earth's magnetic field is decreasing with a half-life of 1465 (plus or minus 165) years. This means that after 1465 years, the field strength is half as strong. Then, after another 1465 years, its strength again decreases by one half. At this rate, it should decrease to zero in only thousands of years. Evolutionary theories explaining this rapid decrease, as well as how the earth could have maintained its magnetic field for billions of years, are very complex and inadequate.

A much better theory exists within creation science. It is straightforward and based on sound physics, and it explains many features of the field. This theory matches paleomagnetic, historic, and present data, most startlingly with evidence for rapid changes. The word *paleo-magnetic* refers to magnetic signatures in rocks, including microscopic metal-rich grains that are oriented within the rock according to the pattern of a magnetic field that existed when the rock was hardening from a molten state. They are like tiny compass needles locked inside the rock. They provide clues to the direction and strength of the magnetic field that surrounded them when the rock formed. The main result is that the field's total energy (not surface intensity) has always decayed at least as fast as now. At that rate the field could not be more than 20,000 years old.

Many strata are too tightly bent.

In many mountainous areas, strata thousands of feet thick are bent and folded into hairpin shapes. The conventional geologic time scale says these formations were deeply buried and solidified for hundreds of millions of years before they were bent. Yet the folding occurred without cracking, with radii so small that the entire formation had to be still wet and unsolidified when the bending occurred. This implies that the folding occurred less than thousands of years after deposition.

CARBON-DATING AN AMMONITE FOSSIL

Coal, oil, and diamonds contain carbon, so they are logical materials in which to search for the presence of carbon 14, a radioactive carbon isotope that naturally decays into stable nitrogen atoms in thousands of years. If the materials are only thousands of years old, they should still have carbon 14 in them. This has indeed been confirmed by both Bible-believing and nonbelieving scientists.

Another place to look for the carbon 14 young-age indicator is in fossils. Most fossils are seashells, which are made of a mixture of hard mineral and tiny, ropy proteins. Proteins have carbon in their chemical makeup. Now that original (not mineralized) proteins have been discovered in fossils, it stands to reason that many fossil shells might still contain intact protein that could be recovered upon removal of the mineral component.

In 2008, creation geologist Andrew Snelling did just that. He submitted ammonite fossil shells collected near Redding, California, to a standard carbon 14 analysis laboratory. Ammonites were shell-forming creatures that shared a general body plan with such creatures as the squid and chambered nautilus. The lab detected plenty of carbon 14. The amount of carbon 14 still in the shells, taken with assumptions about the relative amounts of carbon 14 in the ancient atmosphere and the ancient ammonite, produced a "carbon age" of between 32,000 and 42,000 years.[1]

Clearly, these fossils cannot be 112 million years old, the age assigned to the rock layer from which they were collected!

Biological material decays too fast.

Natural radioactivity, mutations, and decay degrade DNA and other biological material rapidly. Lab experiments have repeatedly shown that DNA cannot exist in natural environments longer than 10,000 years, yet intact strands of DNA appear to have been recovered from fossils allegedly much older, such as "Neanderthal" bones, insects in amber, and possibly even dinosaur fossils. Bacteria allegedly 250 million years old apparently have been revived with no DNA damage. Original soft tissue, partly decayed proteins, whole blood cells, skin cells, bone cells and other structures from dinosaurs and other creatures have astonished experts.

> Original soft tissue, partly decayed proteins, whole blood cells, skin cells, bone cells and other structures from dinosaurs and other creatures have astonished experts.

Unique fossil pockets around the world hold original soft-tissue fossils. More of these amazing finds are described later in this chapter.

Each of them cannot reasonably be more than thousands of years old. This means that each rock layer that contains them must also be thousands of years old.

There is too much carbon 14 in deep geologic strata.

With their short 5700-year half-life, no carbon 14 atoms should exist in any isolated carbon sample older than 250,000 years. Yet it has proven impossible to find any natural source of carbon below Pleistocene (Ice Age) strata that does not contain significant amounts of carbon 14 even though such strata are supposed to be millions or billions of years old. Conventional carbon 14 laboratories have been aware of this anomaly since the early 1980s, have striven to eliminate it, and are unable to account for it. The world's best laboratory, which has learned during two decades of low carbon 14 measurements how not to contaminate specimens externally, under contract to creation scientists, confirmed such observations for coal samples and even for a dozen diamonds, which cannot be contaminated *in situ* with recent carbon. These constitute very strong evidence that the earth is only thousands, not billions, of years old.

Diamonds have too much carbon 14.

Natural diamonds are believed to have been formed deep underground in the upper mantle of the earth's crust. Under extreme temperature and pressure, pure carbon is formed into the diamond's crystalline form. Over time, the diamond is moved upward by rising magma. Natural diamonds are commonly believed to have been formed millions of years ago.

Here is a significant problem for the supposed long ages: Carbon 14 has been measured within natural diamonds. But if the rate that carbon 14 decays has been consistent, any carbon 14 older than 100,000 years is undetectable by current measuring techniques.

And yet carbon 14 is present within natural diamonds. That means the decay rate of carbon 14 is not uniform, or the diamonds are younger than believed, or both. Carbon 14 in diamonds is evidence that the earth is thousands of years old, not millions.

CARBON DATING A MOSASAUR FOSSIL

In 2011, a group of evolutionary scientists based in Sweden carbon-dated mosasaur bone proteins. Mosasaurs are extinct marine reptiles that swam like sharks and grew to more than 45 feet long. Like seashell material, bone is made of both minerals and proteins. The researchers found abundant original collagen protein fibers inside the mosasaur bone.

Their intention was not to carbon-date the creature, which they insisted was 70 million years old, but to rule out recent fungal growth or preparatory glue as possible sources of the carbon. They argued that the carbon source was not fungus or glue because these would have been added to the fossil much more recently than 24,000 years. Thus, the carbon must have come from the intact bone collagen. And based on these carbon 14 results, the original mosasaur's collagen carbon can be no older than 24,000 years![2]

Minerals have too much helium.

Granite is one of the more common rock formations on the earth. The shiny black specks in granite are called *mica*. Within mica are natural zircon crystals, only a few microns in size. As the zircon crystals form, they capture uranium and thorium atoms inside the crystal. Uranium and thorium generate helium atoms as they decay to lead. Helium quickly diffuses out of zircon.

A study published in the *Journal of Geophysical Research* showed that such helium produced in zircon crystals in deep, hot pre-Cambrian granitic rock has not had time to escape. Though the rocks supposedly contain 1.5 billion years' worth of nuclear-decay products, newly measured rates show that helium from zircon has been leaking for only a few thousand years.

If the granite is millions of years old, as commonly believed, all the helium should be gone. However, measurements indicate that much of the helium still remains. Either the diffusion rate of the helium is not uniform, the zircon crystals are younger than believed, or both. This is evidence not only for the youth of the earth but also for episodes of greatly accelerated decay rates of long half-life nuclei within thousands of years, compressing radioisotope timescales enormously.

Helium in granite is evidence that the earth is thousands of years old, not millions.

The sea floor doesn't have enough mud.

Each year, water and wind erode about 20 billion tons of dirt and rock from the continents and deposit it in the ocean. This material accumulates as loose sediment on the hard basaltic (lava-formed) rock of the ocean floor. The average depth of all the sediment in the whole ocean is less than 400 meters. The main way known to remove the sediment from the ocean floor is by plate tectonic subduction. That is, the sea floor slides slowly (a few centimeters each year) beneath the continents, taking some sediment with it. According to secular scientific literature, that process presently removes only 1 billion tons per year. As far as anyone knows, the other 19 billion tons of mud per year simply accumulates. At that rate, erosion would deposit the present mass of sediment in less than 12 million years.

Yet according to evolutionary theory, erosion and plate subduction have been going on as long as the oceans have existed, an alleged 3 billion years. If that were so, the oceans would be massively choked with sediment dozens of kilometers deep. An alternative explanation from creation science is that erosion from the waters of the Genesis flood running off the continents deposited the present amount of sediment within a short time about 5000 years ago.

The sea does not have enough minerals.

Every year, salt accumulates in the ocean from rivers. Given the present rate it is increasing per year, the current 3.5 percent salinity of seawater is much too low if this process has been going on for a very long time.

Measurement "Clocks" and Unprovable Assumptions

Determining with certainty any date prior to the beginning of historical records is impossible—except, of course, by divine revelation. Science, in the proper sense, is based on observation, and we have no past records of observation except historical records. Natural processes can be used to estimate prehistoric dates but not to determine such dates. The accuracy of the estimates will depend on the validity of the assumptions applied to the processes in making such calculations.

Any geochronological calculation is based on at least three assumptions:

- constant process rate (or known functional variation of process rate)

- closed process system (or known external effects on the open system)

- initial process components known

If the assumptions are reasonable and confirmed by observation, a natural process can provide age range estimates that are beyond reasonable doubt. However, if the assumptions are wrong, the clock is invalid. For example, one must assume that the clocklike process has been operating consistently over time, and one must also assume something about the starting conditions.

The magnitude of the error in the assumptions will obviously vary quite widely from process to process, so one would expect to get a wide range of apparent ages from different processes. Also, one cannot be certain about any geochronological calculation, and all are subject to error. The calculations necessary to arrive at origin dates involve some 76 different processes for calculating the age of various integral parts of the earth. All of them yield an age of much less than the present standard evolutionary estimate of approximately 4.5 billion years.

Summarizing the Evidence

- Continent-sized rock layers resulted from the Genesis flood.

- Fossils form fast from catastrophes.

- Many natural processes clearly indicate that the earth is not billions, but thousands of years old.

Biblical Insight

Study 2 Peter 3:4-7.

1. What historical events did Peter warn his readers that scoffers would willfully ignore?

2. Compare this with Isaiah 28:14-15.

3. What are the "scoffers" in both passages trying to avoid by ignoring these events?

6

Evidence from Life Science

And the LORD God formed man of the dust of the
ground, and breathed into his nostrils the breath
of life; and man became a living soul.

Genesis 2:7

Creation and evolution, between them, exhaust the possible
explanations for the origin of living things. Organisms either
appeared on the earth fully developed or they did not. If they did
not, they must have developed from pre-existing species by some
process of modification. If they did appear in a fully developed
state, they must have been created by some omnipotent intelligence.

D.J. Futuyma

Life Could Not Just Happen

There were no human witnesses to the origin of life, and
no physical geologic evidence of its origin exists. That pretty
well summarizes the extent of the progress evolutionists have made
toward establishing a mechanistic, atheistic scenario for the origin of
life after more than half a century of physical, chemical, and geologic
research.

We can, however, derive facts that establish beyond doubt that an
evolutionary origin of life on this planet would have been impossible.
The origin of life could only have resulted from the action of an intelligent agent external to and independent of the natural universe.

The phenomenon of life did not develop by natural processes from
inanimate systems. The first human beings were specially created in

fully human form from the start. Biological life was specially and super-naturally created by the Creator. Here are a few of the insuperable barriers to an evolutionary origin of life.

The required atmosphere was absent.

Our present atmosphere consists of 78 percent nitrogen (N_2), 21 percent molecular oxygen (O_2), and 1 percent other gases, such as carbon dioxide (CO_2), argon (Ar), and water vapor (H_2O). An atmosphere containing free oxygen would be fatal to all origin-of-life schemes. Oxygen is necessary for life, but free oxygen would oxidize and thus destroy all organic molecules required for the *origin* of life. We have much evidence that the earth has always had a significant quantity of free oxygen in the atmosphere, but evolutionists persist in declaring that there was no oxygen in the earth's early atmosphere.

However, this too would be fatal to an evolutionary origin of life. Without oxygen, there would be no protective layer of ozone surrounding the earth. The deadly ultraviolet light from the sun would pour down on the surface of the earth unimpeded, destroying the organic molecules required for life, reducing them to simple gases, such as nitrogen, carbon dioxide, and water.

Evolutionists face an irresolvable dilemma. In the presence of oxygen, life could not evolve; without oxygen, thus no ozone, life could not evolve or exist near the planet's surface.

All forms of raw energy are destructive.

The energy available on a hypothetical primitive earth would consist primarily of radiation from the sun, with some energy from electrical discharges (lightning) and minor sources of energy from radioactive decay and heat.

The problem for biochemical evolution is that the sources of raw energy destroy biological molecules much faster than they form them. The rapid decomposition of those supposed building blocks of life would eliminate any possibility of them accumulating enough organic compounds regardless of how much time might be available.

Even if the "primitive" ocean was chock-full of organic compounds, the proven principles of chemical thermodynamics and kinetics would eliminate even the possibility of lifeless suspended particles forming.

An evolutionary origin of life would result in nothing but clutter.

Let's suppose for a moment that organic, biologically important molecules could have somehow formed in a significant quantity on a primitive earth. An indescribable mess would have been the result.

In addition to the 20 different amino acids found in proteins today, hundreds of other kinds of amino acids would have been produced. In addition to the five-carbon sugars found in DNA and RNA today, a variety of other five-carbon, four-carbon, six-carbon, and seven-carbon sugars would have been produced. In addition to the five specific nucleic acid chemical bases required in DNA and RNA, a large number of other, biologically meaningless bases would exist.

The amino acids in proteins are exclusively left-handed, but all amino acids on the primitive earth would be 50 percent left-handed and 50 percent right-handed. The sugars in DNA and RNA today are exclusively right-handed, but if they existed on a primitive earth, they would have been 50 percent right-handed and 50 percent left-handed. If just one right-handed amino acid is in a protein, or just one left-handed sugar is found in a DNA or RNA, all biological activity is destroyed.

No mechanism would be available on a primitive earth to select the correct form. This fact alone destroys evolution. All these many varieties would compete with one another, and a great variety of other organic molecules, including aldehydes, ketones, acids, amines, lipids, and carbohydrates would exist. Evolutionists have been wrestling with this dilemma since it was first recognized, and no solution is in sight.

Micromolecules do not spontaneously combine to form macromolecules.

The formation of a molecule requires the input of a highly selected type of energy and the steady input of the building blocks required to form it. To produce a protein, the building blocks are amino acids. For DNA and RNA, these building blocks are nucleotides, which are composed of purines, pyrimidines, sugars, and phosphoric acid. If amino acids are dissolved in water, they do not spontaneously join together to make a protein. That would require an input of energy. If proteins are dissolved in water, the chemical bonds between the amino acids slowly break apart, releasing energy.

To form a protein in a laboratory, the chemist must dissolve the required amino acids in a solvent and then add a chemical that contains high-energy bonds. The energy from this chemical is transferred to the amino acids. This provides the necessary energy to form the chemical bonds between the amino acids and releases hydrogen and oxygen to form water. This happens only in a chemistry laboratory or in the cells of living organisms. It could never have taken place in a primitive ocean or anywhere else on a primitive earth.

Evolutionists persistently claim that the initial stage in the origin of life was the origin of a self-replicating DNA or RNA molecule. There is no such thing as a self-replicating molecule, and no such molecule could ever exist.

> There is no such thing as a self-replicating molecule,
> and no such molecule could ever exist.

CELLULAR BUILDING BLOCKS FROM OUTER SPACE?

Perhaps no other realm of investigation has suffered from as much disappointment as the search for nature-only ways to convert raw chemicals into a reproducing cell. The level of desperation among these researchers is evident in the amount of imagination required to concoct solutions to this intractable evolutionary dilemma.

For example, serious scientists will sometimes admit that life must have come from another planet because they know it could not have resulted from any earthbound conditions. Atoms and physics are the same everywhere, so almost any life-friendly set of conditions can be arranged in laboratories, and none of them show the slightest glimmer of hope for life from soup. And there is no scientific evidence that life anywhere but the earth would be possible.

Periodically, biochemicals are discovered in meteorites, and we soon find articles with titles like this: "Life Elements Came from Space."[1] But in every case, further research shows such discoveries to be irrelevant to the problem, and many of them fail to adequately rule out the strong possibility that the biochemicals entered the meteorites after they had been lying on the ground.

Most origin-of-life research is focused on obtaining just the basic chemicals of life— some of which do not form under any lab conditions. Many turn a blind eye to an equally impossible problem—obtaining just the right information required to arrange those basic chemicals into life-sustaining molecular machines. No wonder that even outspoken God-haters admit, "The most profound unsolved problem in biology is the origin of life itself."[2]

Of course the problem *has* been solved. All the evidence shows that only God could have created life. Who is willing to follow the evidence where it leads?

DNA could not survive without repair mechanisms.

DNA, messenger RNA, transfer RNA, and ribosomal RNA are destroyed by a variety of agents, including ultraviolet light, reactive oxygen species, alkylating agents, and water. Yes, even water is one of the agents that damages DNA! Thus water and many chemical agents dissolved in it, along with ultraviolet light, would destroy DNA much faster than it could be produced by the wildest imaginary process.

Researchers have found 130 human DNA repair genes and expect to find more. If it were not for DNA repair genes, DNA could not survive even in the protective environment of a cell. How then could DNA survive when subjected to brutal attack by all the chemical and other DNA-damaging agents that would exist on the hypothetical primitive earth?

DNA is necessary for the survival of DNA! Therefore, DNA repair genes could not have evolved before ordinary DNA, and ordinary DNA could not have evolved before DNA repair genes. This is another impossible barrier for evolution.

The natural direction of life is degeneration, not evolution.

Damage to the genome shortens the lifespan of both individuals and entire populations. As time passes, genetic information erodes.

Mutations in the genomes of organisms are typically nearly neutral, with little effect on the fitness of the organism. However, deleterious (harmful) mutations do accumulate, and this process leads to genetic degeneration. Mutations lead to the loss of genetic information and consequently the loss of genetic potential.

This results in *genetic load* for a population of organisms. Genetic load is the amount of mutation in a kind of organism that affects its fitness for a particular environment. As genetic load increases, the fitness decreases, and the organism progresses towards extinction as it is unable to compete with other organisms for resources, such as food and living space.

An increase in genetic potential through mutation has not been observed, but the increase in genetic load through mutation is observable in all organisms, especially in man.

Life Was Created Fully Functional and Immutable

Given all the reasons why no evolutionary or purely naturalistic scenario could explain the origin of life, the most logical inference is that life was created by an omnipotent and omniscient First Cause that transcends our universe.

DNA was created as a reservoir for the information of life.

The complex language system that stores life's blueprints demands an author. For life to exist, an information system is needed to produce and regulate life functions. This information system must also be able to accurately copy itself for the next generation. Deoxyribonucleic acid (DNA) is the information system for life.

The complex language system that stores
life's blueprints demands an author.

Information is a product of intelligence, indicating that DNA came from an intelligent source (the Creator).

DNA was created with the information to produce proteins for cellular reactions and the ability to copy itself. DNA uses an intermediate, RNA (ribonucleic acid), to transfer this information to the cell machinery to form proteins.

There are several layers of information in DNA. DNA has the genetic code, or code of life, to spell out proteins, but the code is also arranged to minimize errors in protein sequence and structure, regulate the amount of proteins produced in the cell, and assist proteins in folding into the correct shape.

Changes in the information in DNA are called *mutations*, and they adversely affect the cell and organism.

Proteins were created to catalyze the reactions of life.

Life requires not only information but also the ability to control or catalyze chemical reactions. Proteins known as enzymes do this for all living things. Without enzymes, life would not be possible, even in the presence of DNA.

Proteins are formed from long chains of amino acids. Approximately 20 different amino acids are found in living systems. Several important characteristics indicate that protein formation from amino acids requires information. Amino acids in living systems are all left-handed, a property called *chirality*. Amino acids must also be activated in order to be linked together to form proteins. Activation requires more enzymes to form the amino acid chains necessary to make proteins. Proteins must also be folded into the correct shape or they will not be functional, requiring additional information for the correct shape for a specific protein.

DNA and proteins work together to make a cell function normally. Mutations can lead to changes in the amino acid sequence in proteins. Just one change in the amino acid sequence in a protein can cause diseases, such as cystic fibrosis and sickle-cell anemia. These mutations do not lead to more advanced organisms but to organisms that are less fit for survival.

Cells protect life systems.

Cells represent the very existence of physical life and come from similar preexisting life. For DNA and proteins to function properly, a barrier must surround these molecules to prevent unwanted reactions with the chemicals in the environment. As expected, DNA has the information to maintain this barrier, the cell membrane, and proteins provide the catalyst for carrying out the reactions necessary for building and maintaining this barrier. Information in DNA also constructs the cell membrane so that it selects substances useful to the cell and protects against those that will cause harm. These three factors— DNA information, protein catalysts (enzymes), and a protective environment—are all required simultaneously for life to exist as cells.

> Three factors—DNA information, protein catalysts (enzymes), and a protective environment—are all required simultaneously for life to exist as cells.

Cells also represent the very existence of physical life, an observation that led to the cell theory.

All living things are made of cells.

All cells come from similar preexisting cells.

Cells perform the functions of all living things.

From this simple observation, it is clear that life comes from similar preexisting life (a theory called *biogenesis*) and not from nonliving material or unrelated life forms. Scripture tells us that ultimately all life originated from Christ (John 1).

Only God could have made cells.

The minimum requirements for physical cellular life are numerically vast, information rich, and structurally precise. Natural processes are not known to generate any of the kinds of molecular machines—many of which can manipulate specific, single atoms—that are required to sustain cells. Nor is there any plausible scenario yet imagined whereby the laws of chemistry and physics alone could manufacture the very mechanisms that enable living things to avoid the natural consequences of those laws—decay and diffusion.

The higher the number of specifications required for life, the lower the probability that life could have arisen through random, undirected forces. The actual number of specifications now known is so high that there is no reasonable doubt that life must have been engineered by a perceptive power that exists beyond natural laws. Natural entities cannot account for life, so a supernatural entity must.

This conclusion is consistent with biblical creation. For example, Revelation 4:11 states, "Thou art worthy, O Lord, to receive glory and honor and power: for thou hast created all things, and for thy pleasure they are and were created."

Those who reject the Bible continue to research possible ways that nature could have generated a living cell. After almost a century of effort, and even using intricately designed experimental setups, they have met with total failure in producing even the most basic chemicals used as building blocks for the larger chemicals of living cells. God—not nature—made life, so these evolutionary efforts will continue to fail.

> God—not nature—made life, so these evolutionary efforts will continue to fail.

God's design is an engineering wonder.

Some natural systems, especially living systems, contain ingenious solutions for solving technical problems. Human inventors must solve the same physical problems in order to achieve similar results, and therefore many people are taking inspiration from preexisting devices found in nature. This practice, called *biomimicry*, ranges from the simple—like the antiglare smudges under football players' eyes, a tactic taken from raccoons and meerkats—to the complex, such as reflective-lens technology on satellite telescopes, borrowed from certain lobster eyes.

Evolutionary philosophy holds that ingenious biological features were invented by the unknowing, uncaring, purposeless laws of nature, but it is clear that they were instead engineered by our wise, benevolent, and powerful Creator. Nature has never been observed inventing these kinds of complex structures, each well-suited to its task, and there is no theoretical, realistic, step-by-step evolutionary explanation for how they could have developed. Thus, in the same way that we infer a painter from a painting or an engineer from an engine, we infer a Creator from a creation.

The design features that God programmed into natural systems enable their possessors to overcome the limitations imposed on them by the very laws of nature that some people believe are responsible for their development. These features are so finely tuned to perform their tasks that they are used as models for human inventors to follow. It stands to reason, then, that God the Creator deserves unending credit as the ultimate inventor.

Natural selection and adaptation only preserve life forms.

Changes in basic kinds are limited to variations within the kinds. Harmful mutations lead to extinction, not to new complex systems. Mutations cannot create a single gene.

Plants and animals were originally created with large gene pools and the ability to adjust certain features between generations. These capabilities give a created kind the genetic potential to adapt to various ecosystems and help ensure its survival.

This capacity to adapt and survive does not appear to be driven primarily by natural selection, a Darwinian concept that proposes that variations to an organism's features are culled and sorted by external environmental factors. Instead, the capacity to adapt may most often derive from a creature's innate genetic programming. This is what one would expect if the Creator had outfitted His creatures with the tools to perform His directive to "multiply and fill the [ever-changing] earth."

Consider dog breeds. There are many shapes, sizes, and colors of dogs, illustrating the tremendous genetic potential in this kind of animal. Other kinds of plants and animals have similar potential to produce variety within a created kind. Some varieties more readily survive in certain environments and thus more easily pioneer those places. This requires the genetic material already present in organisms. Thus, perhaps the phrase *natural selection* should be replaced with a phrase like *programmed filling* to more accurately describe the interface between organisms and the environment.

Creatures generate new trait varieties, and groups of creatures have been killed by lethal conditions, but no creature has ever been observed changing into another created kind.

> No creature has ever been observed
> changing into another created kind.

Living creatures were clearly designed.

Some of the same attributes seen in man-made tools are also found in living organisms. When parts fit well together, depend on each other, and interact to achieve a purpose, they can be recognized as a designed system. This recognition enables the practice of archaeology and forensics. Generally, the more specified and complex the parts of a system are, the more numerous they are. The more efficient the system is, the more engineering skill and knowledge were required to form that system.

Some of the same attributes required of the designer of a man-made machine, such as a camera—intelligence, purposeful intent, knowledge of the materials and physical principles involved, and the like—must also be required of the One who designed complex biological features, such as the vertebrate vision system. Scripture confirms that enough of the attributes of God are known to all men through what He has made that "they are without excuse" if they choose to ignore Him (Romans 1:20).

Clear examples of design in living creatures abound. One is the tendon that emerges from a chest muscle in most birds. It is threaded through a hole in the bird's bone, wraps around a "pulley," and attaches to the top of the humerus bone. This way, when the muscle flexes, the wing moves up. Each specification involved is exactly fitted to perform its needed function. If only one of them failed to work, the bird would not fly.

In recent decades, the incredible world of tiny machines inside living cells has been revealed. It demonstrates a supremely efficient, and in many cases perfectly specified, collection of parts upon which each living cell depends. Large creatures were clearly designed, but it is even more certain that single cells must have had a Designer of unsurpassed engineering genius. There is no such thing as a simple living organism.

Man was recently and miraculously created in the image of God.

The first human beings did not evolve from an animal ancestry, but were specially created in fully human form from the start.

What separates man from the animal kingdom? Human genetics and appearance are different from those of any animal. But even though man's genome is the most obvious clue to his unique nature, other less apparent signs are even more important.

Genesis 1 reveals that man was created in the image of God, a quality that separates him from the animals. This special creation explains why man's behavior is far more complex than that of any other living thing on the planet. Man reveals God's image in many ways, including his ability to...

- imagine and make objects never seen before
- show compassion for strangers
- ponder his role and fate in creation

Mankind also differs from the other creatures in his relationship to God. People were created to serve God and others, a fact that forms the basis for society. We are God's most treasured creation. God esteems us so much that He died to reconcile us to Himself. This value that God places on us is what truly separates us from the rest of creation. What really distinguishes people from animals is the decision each person will make in response to God's provision for salvation.

> What really distinguishes people from the animals is the decision each person will make in response to God's provision for salvation.

All people descended recently from a single family.

The first human beings, Adam and Eve, were specially created by God, and all other men and women are their descendants. Mitochondria (certain parts of every human cell) carry a small amount of DNA. Mitochondria are inherited solely through the egg from the mother, allowing the identification of descendants from any female lineage. Variations in mitochondrial DNA between people have conclusively shown that all people can trace their mitochondrial ancestry back to a single female, just as it is stated in Scripture.[3]

Fathers pass Y chromosomes to their sons, and just as mitochondrial DNA shows that all have descended from one female, Y chromosome analysis suggests that all men have descended from one common male ancestor.[4]

Humans are stewards with purpose and accountability.

Mankind was instructed to care for all other created organisms and for the earth itself. We fulfill the Creator's commission through science, technology, commerce, fine art, and education. Man has dominion over the earth, but that dominion cannot exceed the boundaries of God's laws. We are stewards of God's creation.

Responsible environmental management includes preservation of the ecosystem and provision for basic human needs. This responsibility includes avoiding reproductive technologies that intentionally destroy human life or create human life for experimentation. It also includes using biotechnology to provide relief from human suffering but avoiding human genetic or cybernetic enhancements that provide super-human qualities.

Christ left an example by relieving human suffering around Him without providing enhancement to those who were not in need of healing. He did these things to bring glory to God and to reveal Himself as God's Son. He never performed miracles to glorify the disciples or others who surrounded Him. The disciples followed this example, and when they healed someone, they acknowledged God as the Deliverer.

Man was created distinct from apes.

Decisive evidence has accumulated that refutes the evolutionary concept that mankind evolved from an apelike ancestor. For example, all candidate intermediate forms are disputed by evolutionary paleontologists.[5] A fossil thought by some evolutionists to represent a prehuman is often interpreted by others as an extinct primate.

Also, none of the proposed transitional forms possess features that show any half-developed structures. Instead, the features are all already fully formed and suited for the individual's overall mode of life, whether living in trees or dwelling on the ground. Further, nobody has demonstrated step-by-step how any apelike set of features could have transmuted into any of the long list of specifically human traits, including skeletal arrangements that enable mankind's peculiar and efficient manner of walking with his knees pointed forward.

The Creator of all life said in His Word that He created mankind specially and in His image, and the fossil evidence bears this out. Some fossils are not informative enough to accurately identify. Thus, hominid fossils are either from humans or from apes.

Issues of Death

"The last enemy that shall be destroyed is death" (1 Corinthians 15:26).

"Death is the essential condition of life, not an evil" (Charlotte Perkins Gilman).

These quotations encapsulate the core debate between the naturalistic worldview and the creationist worldview. According to evolutionary naturalists, death is a good and essential mechanism to continue the movement of time. By contrast, the Bible defines death as an enemy and the result of God's judgment on Adam for his rebellion. God's good creation was cursed by death, which "passed upon all men" (Romans 5:12).

Charlotte Perkins Gilman (1860–1935) was an ardent American Darwinist, utopian feminist, evolutionary humanist, and a prolific writer of novels, short stories, poetry, nonfiction, and social reform lectures. Her sociology heavily impacted early twentieth-century thinking. Sadly, her view of death as an essential condition of life has been embraced by many in the theological world.

Did God design eons of death into the creation?

Some have suggested that all living things were originally designed by God to die, that over the millions of years in which animal and prehuman life was developing, death played a perfectly natural role in the creation. Some have even taught that the death with which God threatened Adam was a special kind of death that applied only to humans.

Necessary death and long ages are exactly what atheistic science would advocate. But how can the God who is life create death as part of His own signature? How ludicrous to think God would design death into His creation and then agonize over the necessity of His own death in order to bring us salvation. Death by the design of God is absolutely foreign to the revealed nature of God (Romans 1:20).

> How can the God who is life create death
> as part of His own signature?

In Genesis 3—the turning point in Scripture—God instantly withdrew all of the good in creation, and by His word He activated the groaning and travailing of the earth and its inhabitants (Romans 8:22-23). The ground was cursed, yielding thorns and thistles, surrounding Adam with sorrowful labor for the rest of his life until he himself would return to the earth from which he was fashioned.

But was God lying? Was He now blaming Adam for what He Himself had done? If the death pronounced by God is nothing more than a symbol of a greater message, then death can be relegated to a mystical musing that has no tangible meaning.

Is physical death irrelevant for salvation?

A dangerous extension of the naturalist's understanding of death is that physical death is essentially irrelevant in the punishment of sin. Gethsemane's agonizing was for nothing, and the hundreds of warnings, curses, and consequences detailed in Scripture are now twisted into allegorical advice or suggestions.

However, physical death is specifically identified as absolutely necessary to accomplish the atonement for sins (Hebrews 9:22). If the "blood of Jesus Christ his Son cleanseth us from all sin" (1 John 1:7; see also Ephesians 1:7; Hebrews 9:14; 1 Peter 1:19), how is it possible to separate this formal and demanding requirement from physical death? Jesus put on flesh and blood only because we are flesh and blood, and by this means He brought reconciliation through His death on the cross (Hebrews 2:14-18), thereby destroying the devil's power of death.

If eons of pain, suffering, and death existed before Adam's awful rebellion brought death into the world, the suffering of our Lord Jesus becomes unnecessary. If the "wages of sin" (Romans 6:23) is nothing more than some sort of spiritualized distance from the Creator, the entire burden of sin becomes nothing more than a mental attitude. Heaven and hell are whatever you make of them.

Twisting the words of Scripture so that Christ's physical death had no meaning is a terrible heresy.

Biological Clocks Indicate Recent Creation

In addition to a wide range of natural processes from astronomy and geology that show a young universe, biological systems also most easily fit within a history measured in the thousands of years rather than millions.

Mutational buildup indicates living populations are young.

DNA carries vital instructions for the maintenance and reproduction of cellular life. Mutations are copy errors that degrade this information. All creatures experience mutations. Very rarely, a mutational error can help some individuals in a population survive in an unusual environment. A mutation can cause disease or death, but the vast majority of mutations have no effect on the organism. They are too subtle to cause a difference in any trait, so no process can detect them. Therefore, these nearly neutral mutations build up relentlessly.

Eventually, the accumulating mutations will damage vital systems and cause *mutational meltdown*, which leads to extinction. The buildup of mutations is accelerated by small population sizes, making recovery difficult or impossible. For example, conservationists must carefully breed pandas, giant salamanders, Tasmanian devils, Bengal tigers, and many more endangered creatures with others of their kinds that have the fewest mutations. But this only delays the inevitable.

With 100 mutations per 20-year generation, the human genome would not last much longer than 500 generations.[6] Mutational buildup acts as a clock ticking down toward extinction, and many animals have yet to reach that point, so life on earth must be only thousands, not millions, of years old.

> With 100 mutations per 20-year generation, the human genome would not last much longer than 500 generations.

Living fossils display no signs of evolution's long ages.

Sometimes called Lazarus taxa, living fossils are organisms that were thought to be extinct but turn up alive in modern populations. Ranging from magnolia flowers to gar fish, and from single-cell algae filaments to lobsters, the living counterparts look so much like their fossilized predecessors that identification down to the species level is often possible.

One of the most spectacular living fossils is the coelacanth, a lobe-finned fish. Once known only from fossilized remains, this fish was considered by many to be a key transitional form (a "missing link") between fish and amphibians. Its fossils are found in Devonian strata, which are assigned a stunningly vast age of 400 million years. However, a live coelacanth hauled up in a fishing net off Madagascar in 1938 showed the same well-designed form as the fossils. It uses its unique fins to orient itself vertically in the deepest seas of the Indian Ocean, not to walk onto land from shallow waters. Where is any evidence of "natural selection" having made even one significant change in this fish over its supposed 400-million-year existence? A similar question could be asked of a host of living fossils.

The most straightforward explanation for why the living form looks so much like the fossilized one is that instead of eons of evolution having taken place, both were created recently.

Fresh tissues show that fossils are recent.

Paleontologists, operating under the assumption that earth's strata represent millions or billions of years, have not looked for fresh tissues within fossilized remains. But fresh biological material within some fossils has been there all along and is being continually discovered, despite the protests of biochemists that it should not exist.

Telltale molecules (such as proteins, pigments, and DNA), intact cells, and in some cases, even cells still grouped together in tissues have been found in fossils that are supposedly millions of years old. Whole organisms sealed in amber deposits have produced more than a thousand kinds of still-living microbes. Fresh tissues and living cells cannot possibly be millions of years old, and they constitute some of the strongest evidence for the young world that the Bible describes.

SOFT-TISSUE FOSSILS—ONLY IN A YOUNG WORLD

ICR News compiles published discoveries of original soft-tissue fossils at www.icr.org/fresh-fossils. More than 20 soft-tissue fossils are described in those articles, but many more were revealed in technical literature before 2008, when *ICR News* went online. Here is what this remarkable evidence shows.

Biochemists know two fundamental facts about biological

materials, such as proteins, DNA, and sugars. First, if kept nearly sterile, dry, and airtight, some of them can last a few thousand years. For example, the Dead Sea Scrolls are 2000 years old and are primarily made of parchment, which is 95 percent collagen protein.

Second, under those same conditions, those biological materials decay spontaneously into dust in fewer than 30,000 years. This is why the Dead Sea Scroll parchments are now so fragile. Similarly, mummified lizard and dinosaur skin, connective tissue, and even some organs have become quite fragile.

Unique fossil pockets around the world have divulged an array of biomaterials, including pigmented cell features called *melanosomes* (from bird feathers, dinosaur skin, squid ink, and eyes), intact but not mineralized dinosaur ligaments, blood vessels, blood cells, bone cells, arthropod shells, bone and shell collagen protein, and even seeds and leaves from intact intestinal tracts.

These could not have been deposited millions of years ago. They appear just as if they were deposited about 4400 years ago during the Genesis flood.

Summarizing the Evidence

- Formation of a living cell from organic soup is impossible without a powerful Supergenius.

- Science confirms that mankind is totally unique among all creatures and is decaying and genetically disintegrating as a species, not evolving. Mankind was created in the image of God.

- Soft-tissue fossils are perfectly compatible with a recent creation and a recent worldwide flood.

Biblical Insight

All New Testament contributors regarded the Old Testament, including Genesis 1–11, as straightforward history.

1. Compare God's inscription recorded in Exodus 20:11, Jesus' statement in Mark 10:6, Paul's sermon in Acts 17:24-26, and Peter's warning in 2 Peter 3:5-6.

2. At any point, any of these authors could have included the concept of vast time. Why is it never mentioned throughout Scripture?

7

Evidence from Scripture

For ever, O Lord, thy word is settled in heaven. Thy faithfulness is unto all generations: thou hast established the earth, and it abideth.

Psalm 119:89-90

In Scripture we are told of some trusting in God and others trusting in idols, and that God is our refuge, our strength, our defense.

Sir Isaac Newton

 Scripture clearly presents God as the Creator of all things. The opening of Genesis makes this obvious, and the rest of Scripture is replete with the theme that the timeless God of eternity past created the universe.

It is no academic secret that the most vocal proponents of evolutionary naturalism and its sociological exponents are atheistic in theory if not in practice. Modernism, postmodernism, and the many variations of scientism are united in their opposition to the concept of a transcendent Creator God. The very idea of an omnipotent, omniscient Being is completely contrary to naturalism.

The myriad pantheistic and polytheistic religious and spiritual "isms" of history, as well as the New Age proponents of today, all embrace some form of eternal matter with a gradual development of the universe and life over long ages. The academic world has begun to entertain spiritual interpretations of naturalistic science as the evidence for complexity and design grows more and more obvious. Yet it still clings to evolutionary cosmologies.

Once again, we are faced with a philosophy, a certain interpretation of information, that is in diametrical opposition to the revealed text of Scripture. A god who would use the cruel, inefficient, wasteful, death-filled, random, purposeless processes and mechanisms of naturalistic evolution contrasts so radically with the God described in the pages of the Bible that one wonders how the two characters can ever be thought to be in harmony.

We must either resolve the conflict or reject one of the two opposing views.

The Authentic Manuscripts

The Bible's text is inspired by God in a way that used selected humans to write its original words (even to each letter in every word). The result is the precise message that God wants us to know. God also providentially ensured that this Book of books was satisfactorily transmitted and reproduced, so its transmitted text is authentic as well as more plentifully distributed than any other book in earth's history.

The hand-copied manuscripts of the Bible far outnumber those of any other book. The evidence for the Bible's authenticity outweighs that of any other literature of antiquity. Textual analysis begins with historical investigation, starting with the latest documents and working backward. As evidence develops, the data are evaluated against other sources. The record is then checked for consistency of information, and the claims are analyzed as if in a legal case, looking for credible testimony with cross-examination. We have an enormous amount of evidence for authenticity of the biblical manuscripts.

The New Testament was written in the first century AD. Some 20,000 manuscripts are in existence. The earliest textual evidence we have was copied 100 years after the original. Contrast this with other ancient writings.

- Caesar's *Gallic Wars* was written in the first century BC. Only ten manuscripts have survived. The earliest textual evidence we have was copied 1000 years after the original.

- Aristotle's *Poetics* was written in the fourth century BC.

Only five manuscripts remain. The earliest textual evidence we have was copied 1400 years after the original.

Many writings of the Church Fathers quote sections of Scripture. In fact, we could reconstruct the entire New Testament from their writings alone. Millions of man-hours have been spent cross-checking the manuscripts. Only 1 percent of all New Testament words are still questioned, and no questionable passage contradicts any Bible teaching.

The Old Testament has been transmitted to us more accurately than has any other ancient writing of comparable age. The textual evidence is greater for both the Old and New Testaments than for any other ancient document. The ancient scribes were very meticulous. There were only 1200 variant readings of Old Testament words in the Masoritic text (AD 500). Other versions confirm this copy's accuracy:

> the Samaritan Pentateuch (400 BC)
>
> the Greek Septuagint (280 BC)
>
> the Dead Sea Scrolls (100 BC)
>
> the Latin Vulgate (AD 400)

The quotations from pre-Christian writing confirm the text. The New Testament accepts the Old Testament as authentic, confirming the traditional authors, quoting from at least 320 different passages, and confirming the supernatural events cited in the Old Testament.

The Authentic Message

There are more than 3000 religions in the world, all of which claim to teach the way to eternal happiness. It has often been said that each of them provides a different path to the same end and that men are free to choose the path that best suits their own disposition and culture. The Word of God insists that this is not so!

The Bible makes clear that the God of the Bible is the only true God (Isaiah 44:6; 45:5-6) and that Jesus Christ is the only way to God (John 14:6). All other religions stress their own paths, allowing for some other contingency.

The Bible insists that it is the only true revelation, its words are not to be changed (Proverbs 30:5-6; Revelation 22:18-19), and its words are the basis of all judgment (John 12:47-50).

The Bible has a unique account of origins (Genesis 1–11). All others are either evolutionary or pantheistic and begin with matter existing from eternity. The biblical account of origins is unique in both quality and quantity of information.

The Bible has a unique historical basis. Other religions are based on the subjective teachings of their founders. Biblical teachings are based on objective and demonstrable facts: creation, the fall, the flood, and the life of Christ.

Creation was 24/6 and recent.

The most controversial book of the Bible is Genesis, especially the first 11 chapters. Those chapters speak of the creation of the universe, man's fall into sin, Noah's worldwide flood, and the language-altering event at Babel. There is much evidence that these events are historically accurate.

Although some would suggest that the biblical account of creation is either allegorical or analogous to the evolutionary story, the text itself does not permit such an application.

The language of Genesis 1–2 is technically precise and linguistically clear. An unbiased reading reveals that the author is describing a creation process that occurred over six normal days and that involves God's supernatural intervention both to create something from nothing and to make and shape something basic into something more complex.

Three days (day one, day five, and day six) involve creation. Three days (day two, day three, and day four) involve the organization, integration, and structuring of the material created on day one.

Animals and man were created on day five. A special image of God was created on day six that only man has. The movement from simple to complex may appear to follow evolution's theory, but the specific order (water > land > plants > stellar and planetary bodies > birds and fish > land animals > man) clearly does not.

The Hebrew word for day (*yom*) is used some 3000 times in the Hebrew Bible and is almost always used to mean an ordinary 24-hour day-night cycle. On the few occasions where it is used to mean an indeterminate period of time, it is always clear from the context that it means something other than a 24-hour day ("day of trouble," "day of the Lord," "day of battle," and so on). Whenever it is used with an ordinal ("day one" or "the first day"), it always means a specific day, an ordinary 24-hour day.

The language of Genesis 1 appears to have been crafted so that no reader would mistake the words to refer to anything other than an ordinary 24-hour day. The light portion is named day, and the dark portion is named night. "Evening and the morning" obviously refers to day one, day two, and so on. The linguistic formula is repeated for each of the six days—a strange emphasis if the words were to be taken as allegorical or analogous to something other than a day-night cycle.

> The language of Genesis 1 appears to have been crafted so that no reader would mistake the words to refer to anything other than an ordinary 24-hour day.

When God wrote the Ten Commandments with His own finger (certainly the most emphatic action ever taken by God on behalf of His revealed Word), He specifically designated a seventh day to be a Sabbath day (rest day) in memory and in honor of His creative activity of working six days and resting one day (Exodus 20:11). In that context, spoken and written by God Himself, the creation week can mean only a regular week of seven days, one of which is set aside as holy.

Sin caused death.

The biblical record is very precise: Adam's sin introduced death into the world (Genesis 3:17-19; Romans 5:12). Death is now "the last enemy" (1 Corinthians 15:26). Naturalistic interpretations must interpret death as a good mechanism that produces the fittest survivors.

Those who hold to the long ages of formative biology assert that death is a normal part of the original creation. Their position is that the fossil remains are a record of eons of natural development rather than the awful debris of a worldwide, yearlong sentence of destruction executed by an angry Creator.

We have seen, however, that the Bible insists that death is an enemy and a curse pronounced on all creation, including living creatures. That awful judgment was because of Adam's rebellion (1 Timothy 2:14) and was not a part of God's good creation.

Death by God's design is so foreign to the revealed nature of God, one is at a loss to understand why anyone would want to suggest that God included death in His original creation, a creation that was designed to tell us of His invisible nature and Godhead. The whole message of Scripture turns on Genesis 3. All of the good in the environment was withdrawn with God's sentence. The groaning and travailing of creation (Romans 8:22) began at that moment. Otherwise, the words of God Himself are void!

If there were eons of pain, suffering, and death before Adam's rebellion brought death into the world, a whole sweep of biblical teaching is thrown into the black hole of allegory. Hundreds of Bible passages that describe a warning and a bad consequence are twisted to refer to a supposedly normal event. In the Bible, physical death is specifically identified as absolutely necessary to accomplish the atonement for sins.

Without question, the Bible teaches that it was necessary for Jesus Christ to die physically in order to accomplish the payment for our sins (Hebrews 2:14-18). If death is normal and good or merely a spiritual effect, the physical death of Jesus Christ becomes unnecessary and meaningless.

> If death is normal and good or merely a spiritual effect, the physical death of Jesus Christ becomes unnecessary and meaningless.

Redemption is necessary.

The Bible presents a unique plan of redemption. It reveals a unique Savior.

- He was born of a virgin (Isaiah 7:14; Matthew 1:18-25).

- He lived a sinless life (Hebrews 4:14-16).

- He taught as no other man taught (Matthew 7:28-29; John 7:46).

- He willingly died a unique death (Luke 23:46; John 10:17-18).

- He won unique victory over death (Acts 17:31; 1 Corinthians 15:3-8).

The Bible demands a unique salvation.

- Perfect holiness is required (Romans 3:10-18,23; 6:23).

- Substitutionary atonement is the only means of reconciliation (Romans 3:24-26; Hebrews 10:4-14).

- Grace is the only measurement (Romans 11:5-6; Ephesians 2:8-10).

Other religions require some form of works or participation.

Conflicts Between Text and Theology

> All scripture is given by inspiration of God, and is profitable for doctrine, for reproof, for correction, for instruction in righteousness: that the man of God may be perfect, thoroughly furnished unto all good works (2 Timothy 3:16-17).

> Scripture is inerrant, not in the sense of being absolutely precise by modern standards, but in the sense of making good its claims and achieving that measure of focused truth at which its authors aimed.[1]

How are we to deal with these two foundational statements on inspiration? The passage from Paul's letter to Timothy is recorded, of course, in the Holy Bible. The other is from a position paper signed and upheld by many (if not most) evangelical leaders. They are quite different. Which one is to rule our practice?

What can be done to achieve unity or a set of doctrines among

Bible-believing Christians? It is doubtful that theology can do much. One's theological background leads to a bias toward the structure of Scripture, a bias that reinforces the opinions that have been embraced during one's training. That is true for dispensational or covenant or reformed or postmodern or whatever interpretive framework is applied. Interpretation places a filter on the words of Scripture so that one can "rightly divide" (according to one's theology).

Just what liberties or restrictions or guidelines can we agree on about the text, about the Scriptures given by the breath of God? In my mind, it all comes down to how we treat the written words of Scripture. The present debate (and to some degree, the agelong debate) involves three *P*s.

Preservation. Just how much of the present text can we trust to be like the original manuscripts? If only the original manuscripts are inspired (without error), then which words, which manuscript, and which translation can be trusted? This important question continues to create problems among evangelicals.

Precision. Just how inspired is Scripture? Is every word of God pure? Or is only the framework inspired? How must we approach the text? Should we trust only each thought or just each sentence, or is each word, each tense, indeed each letter absolutely accurate? Where does the precision of inspiration start or leave off? This is critical to how we study and evaluate Scripture. It makes a big difference in our conclusions for most passages. If we cannot come to agreement here, we cannot arrive at common conclusions about much in the Scripture—let alone develop a consistent worldview.

Perspicuity. This word is less frequently discussed. The term itself is somewhat vague, although it refers to the quality of clearness or lucidity. The clarity of the message has absolutely no meaning if God has not preserved His precise words. Without confidence in the preservation and precision of Scripture, passages can mean whatever anyone may want them to mean. That seems to be what postmodern theologians and the leaders of the Emergent church suggest.

All of us have been impacted by the arguments we have been exposed to, perhaps more than we realize. It would be good for all of us to reevaluate the way we approach Scripture and attempt to come to an agreement—perhaps even to write a set of tenets that would guide our future discussions. If we cannot agree on how to approach the words of God, we surely will not agree about the words of men.

Accurate Data

The information contained in the Bible is holy, and it is wholly accurate too. When the Bible mentions a scientific topic, it is scientifically accurate. Likewise, the Bible is accurate historically, mathematically, and so on.

The Bible is unique among all books. Its form, structure, and history are all distinctive, but even more important, it claims supernatural superiority over all other communication. It insists on total accuracy for its content and absolute obedience to its commands. No other book is so demanding.

Biblical data is testable.

Historical evidence routinely includes ancient literature, business records, and government documents, analyzed in conjunction with linguistics, geography, and archaeological analysis of physical objects (pottery, coins, remains of buildings, and so on) using the same techniques as forensic science. After many millions of man-hours of research and evidence analysis, archaeology has repeatedly confirmed the reliability of the Bible. The Bible has been proven geographically and historically accurate in the most exacting detail by external evidences.

The Bible is historically accurate.

The biblical record is full of testable historical and archaeological data, unlike the sacred texts of other religions. Wherever such historical information is cited, the data has proven to be precise and trustworthy.

The Bible has proven to be more historically and archaeologically accurate than any other ancient book. It has been subjected to the minutest scientific textual analysis possible to humanity and has been proven to be authentic in every way.

The Bible has become a significant source book for secular

archaeology, helping to identify such ancient figures as Sargon (Isaiah 20:1), Sennacherib (Isaiah 37:37), Horam of Gezer (Joshua 10:33), Hazar (Joshua 15:27), and the nation of the Hittites (Genesis 15:20). The biblical record, unlike other religious books, is historically set, opening itself up for testing and verification.

Two of the greatest twentieth-century archaeologists, William F. Albright and Nelson Glueck, were non-Christian and secular in their training and personal beliefs. Yet they both lauded the Bible as the single most accurate source document from history. Over and over again, the Bible has been found to be accurate in its places, dates, and records of events. No other religious document comes even close.

Nineteenth-century critics denied the historicity of the Hittites, Horites, Edomites, and various other peoples, nations, and cities mentioned in the Bible. Those critics have long been silenced by the archaeologist's spade, and few critics dare to question the geographical and ethnological reliability of the Bible.

The names of more than 40 kings of various countries mentioned in the Bible have all been found in contemporary documents and inscriptions outside of the Old Testament. These references are always consistent with the times and places associated with them in the Bible. No other ancient literature has been even remotely as well-confirmed in accuracy as has the Bible.

The Bible is scientifically accurate.

The Bible is not a science textbook, but it does deal with scientifically relevant issues. Although much controversy surrounds the early chapters of Genesis, empirical (observable, testable, repeatable) science verifies the Bible's information.

Many would suggest that the Bible is an antiquated religious book, filled with scientific fallacies and mistakes. Others believe that the Bible is a book of true religion but that it deals solely with spiritual subjects, with any matters of science and history to be interpreted spiritually or allegorically.

The Bible is either wholly reliable on every subject with which it deals or it is not the Word of God. Although the Bible is obviously not a scientific encyclopedia (otherwise it would be continuously out of date), the Bible does contain all the basic principles upon which true science is built. The Bible abounds with references to nature and natural processes and thus frequently touches on the various sciences.

For instance, there are many passages that deal with principles of hydrology, geology, astronomy, meteorology, biology, physics, cosmology, and the grand principles of the space-mass / energy-time continuum.

Again, if the God revealed in the Bible truly exists, then everything that He reveals must be true.

One often hears of mistakes or errors in the Bible. Seldom, when confronted, is there an example provided. When such alleged errors are cited, they fall into three categories: mathematical rounding, relative motion, or miracles. Obviously, mathematical rounding is both scientific and in constant use today, as is the use of relative motion for all sorts of navigation and distance calculations. And to deny the miraculous is to assume that one is omniscient.

Just as the Bible has become a sourcebook for history and archaeology, it is also a sourcebook for the foundational principles of science. Those who ignore the information of Scripture will be "ever learning, and never able to come to the knowledge of the truth" (2 Timothy 3:7).

To deny the miraculous is to assume that one is omniscient.

Plants and animals are distinct.

In the Creator's design, plants were made for food and animals are living evidence of the Creator's wonder and diversity. There is no hint in the Genesis account that God equated the replicating systems of earth with the living creatures later created on days five and six. Much has been written to justify this equation, but neither the Scriptures nor science supports it. There is a vast difference between the most complex plant and the simplest living organism. If one uses the biblical distinction of blood (Leviticus 17:11) as the wall between plant and animal, the differences are even greater.

There is no question that God created the various categories of grass, herbs, and fruit-bearing plants. The gulf between dirt and plants is huge! No naturalistic scheme can adequately account for such wonder. But according to God's words, they do not have the kind of life that we do. Plants do replicate within their kind, but so do certain crystals and some chemicals. They replicate within kind, but they are nowhere said to possess *chay* ("life") or *nephesh* ("soul"), Hebrew words that describe living things. Job 14:8-10 is cited as evidence that plants die just as people die, but that passage most certainly does not use the words for life. The supposed comparison is really a contrast between plant and man.

The food created by God as a good product and part of the process to maintain life cannot be equated with the awful sentence of death pronounced by the Creator on His creation. Animals and man have life. Plants do not.

WHAT PLANTS PROVIDE

Plants do not have the breath of the spirit of life, but they can reproduce after their kinds, and they do provide exactly what living creatures need. Unlike plants, living creatures have blood to carry the "life of the flesh" (Leviticus 17:11) and nostrils to facilitate the "breath of life" (Genesis 7:22).

Creatures with nostrils and blood were originally designed to consume plants, according to Genesis 1:30. Even today, animals ultimately derive their energy from sugars produced by plants. Those sugars are transported from the gut to the animal's tissues through the blood. The gaseous waste produced by biological burning of those sugars in tissues is carried by that same blood to the lungs to be expelled through the nostrils. And the sugar could never have been metabolized were it not for the oxygen taken in through the nostrils, also carried by blood to mix with the sugars in tissues.

Plants merely need sunlight, air, water, and a few essential minerals to manufacture all their own food. But plants make much more food than they need to sustain their own tissues or to propagate.

For example, many plant seeds do not need the fleshy part of the fruit that surrounds them. The fruit is often loaded with sugars, vitamins, and minerals that perfectly match animal body needs even though the plant itself appears to have no need for them! Plants appear to be designed specifically to provide the nutrients required for animals.

In addition, without plants to provide oxygen, animal life would have no breath. In defiance of evolutionary principles, such as the survival and reproduction of the most fit or species ensuring their own propagation, plants give more than they take.

The flood was global.

The language of Genesis 6–9 demands that the great flood of Noah's day be understood as a planet-covering, geologically destructive, year-long water cataclysm. The flood left enormous evidence that it was global.

There is a great divide between two major systems of belief on the Genesis flood. Some say it is either a purely mythological event or possibly a local or regional flood. Others accept the biblical record of the flood as a literal account of a tremendous cataclysm involving not only a worldwide deluge but also great tectonic upheavals and volcanic outpourings that completely changed the crust of the earth and its topography in the days of Noah.

Jesus Christ believed the Old Testament record of the worldwide flood. Speaking of the antediluvian population, He said, "The flood came, and took them all away" (Matthew 24:39).

Evolutionary anthropologists are convinced that people had spread over the entire earth by the time assigned to Noah in biblical chronology, so an anthropologically universal flood would clearly have to have been a geographically worldwide flood.

The apostle Peter believed in a worldwide hydraulic cataclysm. "The world [Greek, *kosmos*] that then was, being overflowed [Greek *katak-luzo*] with water, perished" (2 Peter 3:6). The world was defined in the previous verse as "the heavens…and the earth." Peter also said that God "spared not the old world, but saved Noah…bringing in the flood [Greek, *kataklusmos*] upon the world of the ungodly" (2 Peter 2:5).

The Old Testament record of the flood, which both Christ and Peter accepted as real history, clearly describes a global event. For example, the record emphasizes that "all the high hills, that were under the whole heaven…and the mountains were covered" (Genesis 7:19-20).

"All flesh died that moved upon the earth…all that was in the dry land" (Genesis 7:21-22), so Noah and his sons built a huge ark to preserve animal life for the postdiluvian world, an ark that had more than ample capacity to carry at least two of every known species of land animal. Such an ark was absurdly unnecessary for anything but a global flood.

God promised, "Neither shall there any more be a flood to destroy the earth" (Genesis 9:11), and He has kept His word for more than 4000 years if the flood indeed was global. Those Christians who say the flood was local are in effect accusing God of lying, for many devastating local floods occur every year.

> Those Christians who say the flood was local
> are in effect accusing God of lying.

Reliable Eyewitnesses

The information available about the 40 authors of the biblical text clearly demonstrates both their historicity and their credibility. Many of these writers were well known in secular history, and many suffered cruelly while defending the accuracy of their material.

The Bible, like many books, was written by eyewitnesses of the events and circumstances they recorded (Luke 1:2; 2 Peter 1:16). That they were trustworthy witnesses is only to be expected because God inspired them to coauthor their respective portions of the Bible. But can we know if the Bible's human coauthors were really reliable eyewitnesses?

The following eyewitness traits are emphasized in common law, in law school, and in the rules of evidence.

Reliable witnesses will evidence honesty by their sincerity of speech and be clearly motivated by a drive to speak the truth. The quality of witnesses' observations can be observed by accurate memory, often evidenced by access to accurate records. The competency of their communication will be demonstrated by their ability to recall and describe observations with accurate information and relevant details. Testimonial consistency is also a key factor in reliability.

Though witnesses will provide idiosyncratic differences due to different perspectives and interests, all Scripture has perfect evidentiary consistency. Matthew, Mark, Luke, John, Paul, Moses, Daniel, Jude, and all of the other Bible's coauthors qualify as impeccably reliable eyewitnesses. Many writers of the Bible suffered cruel treatment or even death for their stand on their witness. Their unshakeable belief that their testimony was so true that it was worth suffering and dying for adds obvious credibility to their writings.

Assessable Results

The Bible stands up to being tested, like an anvil beaten by many hammers. The Bible proves that it is God's Word by its prediction of events that were fulfilled beyond all possible odds and are now documented history, including the prophesied events about Jesus as the predicted Messiah. We also have the witness of lives transformed as only the Bible indicated would occur.

> The Bible stands up to being tested, like an anvil beaten by many hammers.

Transformed lives

History is replete with testimonies of radically changed lives. The

Bible speaks of a "new creature" (2 Corinthians 5:17), "created in righteousness and true holiness" (Ephesians 4:24). Such transformation is classic evidence of the power of God.

The message that permeates the Bible is that all humans are sinful by their nature and conscious action and are under the judgment of a holy and righteous Creator-God, who has willingly offered His own Son as the substitutionary sacrifice for humanity's sentence of eternal death. That salvation transforms! It is a new birth that yields a new creation. Such a supernatural event must transform a life if it is real. Both the Bible and history are replete with such evidence.

- Pagan Abram (later Abraham) believed God (Galatians 3:6) and became the "father of many nations" (Genesis 17:5).

- Banished Jacob (Genesis 27:43) became a prince with the name Israel (Genesis 32:28).

- Joseph, despised and hated by his brothers, became the ruler in Egypt "to save much people alive" (Genesis 50:20).

- Moses the murderer became Moses the deliverer (Exodus 3:10).

- Gideon the fearful became Gideon the mighty man of valor (Judges 6:12).

- Samuel the child became Samuel the judge (1 Samuel 7:15).

- David the shepherd became David the giant-killer (1 Samuel 17:45) and king (2 Samuel 7:8).

- Zacchaeus the dishonest tax collector became Zacchaeus the generous benefactor (Luke 19:8).

- Peter the rough commercial fisherman became a "fisher of men" (Matthew 4:19).

- Saul the self-righteous Pharisee and persecutor of Christians (Acts 9:1-2) became Paul the apostle and teacher of the Gentiles (2 Timothy 1:11).

Every book of the Bible contains records of such transformations, as does every era of history. From the coliseum in Rome and the persecutions during the Middle Ages to the wonderful conversions of the modern-day addicts and social outcasts, as well as the quiet and simple response of the child who seeks to return the love of Jesus, all testify to the transforming power of the gospel.

Accurate predictions

The Bible contains many, many prophetic predictions, most of which are quite detailed. Either they come true or they do not. If one prediction is accurate, it might be called coincidence. When dozens or hundreds come true, the odds become astronomical.

The purpose of biblical prophecy is given in Isaiah 46:9-10: "I am God, and there is none like me, declaring the end from the beginning, and from ancient times the things that are not yet done."

Supernatural predictions are evidence provided to us for verification. Not a single prophecy from the Bible has been proven false. Many prophecies remain in the future, but all that have come to pass have been verified to be true. Thousands of prophecies from the Bible have been fulfilled.

An amazing prophecy is found in Revelation 11:9. In AD 90, the apostle John predicted that many nations would view the same event within a few days' time. Today, billions of people from around the world simultaneously view the same event through mass communication. When the prediction was made, communication and transportation across the Roman Empire took months.

In 332 BC, Alexander the Great conquered the island fortress of Tyre by building a causeway from the ruins of the old city. This fulfilled the prophecy in Ezekiel 26:4-5, written hundreds of years before. At the time of Ezekiel, Tyre was the capital of Phoenicia and the island fortress had not yet been built. Ezekiel predicted, "They shall destroy the walls of Tyrus, and break down her towers: I will also scrape her dust from her, and make her like the top of a rock. It shall be a place for the spreading of nets in the midst of the sea."

Two hundred years later, Alexander scraped away everything, leaving bare rock.

And, of course, there are hundreds of fulfilled prophesies related to the birth, life, death, and resurrection of Jesus Christ.

REMEMBERING PROPHECIES DURING CHRISTMAS AND EASTER

The Lord Jesus fulfilled an array of ancient prophecies during His incarnation, which many Christians celebrate annually at Christmas. The holiday season is therefore a handy time of year to remind ourselves of a hallmark of God: He is all-knowing, so He alone knows the future. Here are a few revelations given about the once-future Christ who came once and promised to return.

- A man, the seed of a woman, would defeat Satan (Genesis 3:15).

- The Promised One would come from Abraham (Genesis 12:3), from Judah (Genesis 49:10), and from David (2 Samuel 7).

- Christ would be born in Bethlehem (Micah 5:2) and minister in Jerusalem (Isaiah 59:20).

- He would be born of a virgin mother (Isaiah 7:14).

- He would receive gifts at His birth (Psalm 72:10-11).

Many other messianic prophecies foretold the means of Christ's death and resurrection, making the Easter season another handy time to reinforce the divine authorship of Scripture.

- Christ's hands and feet would be pierced (Psalm 22:16).

- Christ's triumphal entry would be 483 (360-day) years from the decree to rebuild the city of Jerusalem (Daniel 9:25). The decree was recorded in Nehemiah 2:8 and occurred about 446 BC.

- The Holy One would not remain among the dead, but would escape corruption (Psalm 16:10).

These prophecies were fulfilled in Christ's earthly ministry, and yet more await future fulfillment. According to Psalm 78:4-7, fathers should teach their children what God has done. What better time than holidays for fathers to remind the next generation that the Lord Jesus fulfilled centuries-old prophecies of His birth, death, and resurrection?

Contrasting worldviews

The conflict between good and evil in every culture throughout all recorded time is clearly articulated and explained in the Bible. Buried deep in the human psyche are timeless questions that surface frequently and suddenly throughout one's lifetime. Every person capable of rational thought thinks these things. There are no exceptions or exclusions.

- The question of identity: Who am I?
- The question of purpose: Why am I here?
- Questions about the future and life after death: What is going to happen to me?
- Questions about origins: Where did I come from, and how and when did all this start?

No human being operates without a bias, a predisposition to believe one idea over another. In religious terms, we call that bias *faith*.

The naturalist believes that there is no supernatural force in existence and that man has reached the stage in eternity where he is able to direct the evolutionary development of the universe. The creationist believes that a Creator God exists and that the creatures of that God must seek to understand His will.

The common data that these two believers share will be interpreted in the light of the belief system (or worldview, or faith) that they hold. When we ask the questions that plague our minds (Why is the world so full of evil? Why can't we all get along? Why can't we seem to get enough? Is it always going to be this way?), the answers come from our worldview. What we believe will frame our reactions, our priorities, and our expectations.

The Bible describes the many facets of belief systems (worldviews) in their simplest and most fundament form—as truth or as lie.

The ultimate contrast is between the revelation of the Creator-God who cannot lie (Hebrews 6:18) and the great adversary, Satan, who is the father of all lies (John 8:44). The Bible provides a comprehensive and logically consistent body of answers and explanations to all of the critical worldview issues: who (including Who), what, where, when, how, and why. In fact, the Bible even has an explanation for why we have such different viewpoints on the critical worldview issues. The Bible also predicts cause-and-effect connections between the kind of worldview we have, the kind of actions we take in life, and the impact of those actions, both here and in the hereafter.

> The Bible describes the many facets of belief systems (worldviews) in their simplest and most fundament form—as truth or as lie.

Human stewardship

The first command given to humanity was to rule, subdue, and have dominion over the earth. That delegated authority contains the fundamental warrant for all human endeavors as stewardship over earth. This dominion mandate, found in Genesis 1:26-28 and later repeated and amplified to Noah in Genesis 9:1-7, is still in force as the Creator's authorization for humanity to be the stewards of earth.

The dominion mandate authorizes all honorable human occupations as stewardship under God. God's first command to the man and woman He had created was to exercise dominion "over all the earth"—not a despotic dominion, as some have insinuated, but a responsible stewardship.

In order to subdue the earth, we must first understand its processes. Thus, research is the foundational occupation for fulfilling the divine mandate. Then this knowledge must be applied in technology (engineering, medicine, agriculture, and the like). It must be implemented for use by all (through business and commerce) and transmitted to future generations (by means of education). The creation can also be described and praised in the humanities and fine arts.

The dominion mandate thus authorizes all honorable human occupations as a stewardship under God.

The mandate was reaffirmed to Noah after the flood (Genesis 9:1-10) with the additional institution of human government, a change made necessary by the entrance of sin and death into the world. Thus, all the occupations we now call the social sciences (law, civics, counseling, and so on) have been added to God's authorized vocations.

This all-encompassing command will be part of the great judgment. "The dead were judged out of those things which were written in the books, according to their works" (Revelation 20:12).

Science

The command to subdue the earth requires that we first understand it. The disciplines of science uncover how things work. In order for mankind to subdue the earth and have dominion over it, humanity would eventually have to occupy every region of it. Man is to keep the earth (Genesis 2:15), not exploit and waste its resources. The command to subdue does not imply that the earth is an enemy, but rather that it is a complex and wonderful world and is to be ordered and controlled for man's benefit and God's glory.

To subdue and exercise dominion over the physical and biological creations necessarily implies the development of physical and biological sciences, including physics, chemistry, hydrology, biology, physiology, and ecology. The work involved suggests studying and understanding the created world, or as Kepler and other great scientists have put it, "thinking God's thoughts after Him."

Since sin entered the world, profound changes have taken place in all of God's created domains. The ground itself and the living creatures were cursed (Genesis 3:14,17). The principle of decay and disintegration began to operate in physical systems, and mutations, disease, and death began to debilitate biological systems. Now science must not only explain the function and organization of earth but also attempt to uncover the original designs of those processes and learn how to repair the increasing damage being done.

Factual and quantitative data in all areas of study are accessible to all men with the capacity to pursue them. The interpretive and philosophical applications of such data, however, depend strongly on one's spiritual condition.

Technology

The command to rule requires effective use in the service of mankind. The disciplines of technology involve the development and application of all science.

Obedience to the dominion mandate also requires the concordant development of physical and biological technologies, such as engineering, agriculture, and medicine. These activities under the stewardship of the dominion mandate imply the complementary enterprises of science and technology, research and development, theory and practice, and so on.

Technology, development, and practice suggest the application and utilization of the physical and biological processes and systems, as learned from their scientific study, for the benefit of mankind and the glory of God.

Social sciences have also arisen (such as psychology and sociology), as have the technologies for their implementation in organized human societies (including economics, government, and politics), so these fields now also come within the bounds of the dominion mandate and thus are proper disciplines.

As with scientific research, factual and quantitative data in all areas of study are most accurate and useful in technological development. The interpretive and philosophical applications, however, are either tainted or enhanced by one's spiritual condition.

Commerce

The command to fill the earth also involves distributing useful things to everyone. Distribution is implied in the dominion mandate. Science is charged with the responsibility of researching the forces and processes of the earth to determine how things function. Technology is delegated the task of developing useful tools and techniques for the application of the information gained in research. Commerce (business) is the complementary discipline necessary to distribute these useful things to everyone.

> Science is charged with the responsibility of researching the forces and processes of the earth to determine how things function.

In essence, commerce complies with the mandate to fill the earth. Adam and Eve were placed in the garden and told to "dress and keep" it. They were not told how to do so, only that they were responsible before the Creator to maintain and develop what had been provided for them. As the earth's population grew, it would be necessary to develop skills to make their tools and talents available to others. That procedure in modern terms is commerce.

Scripture includes a number of commerce-related instructions. We are told not to be "slothful in business" but "fervent in spirit; serving the Lord" (Romans 12:11). Someone who is "diligent in his business" will "stand before kings; he shall not stand before mean men" (Proverbs 22:29). In one sense, business (commerce) is the familial responsibility of every person, and we are told to "study to be quiet, and to do your own business, and to work with your own hands" (1 Thessalonians 4:11).

Given the somewhat sordid reputation of business in general, it would be well if all commerce would heed the Golden Rule: "As ye would that men should do to you, do ye also to them likewise" (Luke 6:31). Those words were undoubtedly intended to be implemented by humanity when the mandate to fill the earth was first given.

Education

The knowledge of science, the skills of technology, and the techniques of commerce must be transmitted to others. True knowledge and wisdom, once known, must not be lost or corrupted. Each generation is responsible to transmit its knowledge of truth, undiluted and undistorted, to the succeeding generation. This is the ministry of teaching.

In God's economy, the primary responsibility for educating the young rests on the parents (Deuteronomy 6:6-7; Ephesians 6:4; 2 Timothy 3:15). The churches also bear a complementary and extended responsibility to identify and equip God-called teachers as needed for all aspects of its educational ministries (1 Timothy 3:15). The Scriptures never refer to schools as separate institutions established by God.

That fact does not necessarily mean that parents and pastors have to do all the actual work of teaching. It is certainly appropriate for them to employ qualified tutors and trainers, but the control of the educational process should remain primarily with the home and secondarily with the church.

The gift of teaching is identified in all three Bible lists of the gifts of the Spirit (Romans 12:1-8; 1 Corinthians 12; Ephesians 4:7-16). This gift focuses on the teaching of the Scriptures, of course. However, we must not forget that the Bible provides the framework for all teaching. All physical, biological, and spiritual reality is created and maintained by God in Christ and revealed by the Spirit. All teaching, no matter how profound, attractive, or eloquent, should be tested by its fidelity to the Word of God. Thus, the wonderful threefold goal of teaching must...

- transmit the truth in fullness and purity

- train the student with love and wisdom

- glorify Christ, in whom perfect love and absolute truth will be united forever

Humanities

The recording of man's achievements through literature, drama, art, and the like should all redound to God's glory. The humanities and fine arts are spiritual and emotional extensions of the knowledge and technological state of society. The disciplines of science and technology are mostly grounded in factual and quantitative data, but the further one gets from that which is true to that which is applied, the more likely the sin nature will distort or contaminate the discipline.

That contamination affects the humanities and fine arts in even greater measure. These professions cannot even use the empirical data developed by secular persons, as can be done with the social sciences, because there are practically no empirical data involved in the humanities and fine arts.

In this realm, practically everything is based on either human reasoning or emotions, with the exception of the actual mechanical techniques of writing, composing, painting, or performing. But reasoning and emotions come from the mind and heart which, in the secular person, are without the benefit of the godly mind (2 Corinthians 2:14).

As the world has advanced, the growing secularization of society has increased. This is relatively easy to observe in the great art museums of our large cities. As one moves from the older galleries to the modern galleries, the movement of art from realism to abstract and from godly to profane is easy to see. One does not have to be an art critic to observe the trends.

Perhaps it would be helpful for the Christian to remember 1 Corinthians 10:31: "Whether therefore ye eat, or drink, or whatsoever ye do, do all to the glory of God."

Government and politics

The authorization for capital punishment entails the ultimate oversight of human relations through government, politics, sociology... indeed, all legitimate human endeavors. In God's renewal of the dominion mandate to Noah after the flood (Genesis 9:6-7), man was given the institution of human government, epitomized in the authority to impose capital punishment as the penalty for murder. This ultimate in governmental authority, of course, implies also that human government was now responsible to regulate other human interrelationships as well because uncontrolled, self-centered activities could otherwise quickly lead to violence, murder, and anarchy.

Law defines how governments and people should interact. Almost all laws are derived from the Ten Commandments, either directly or in extrapolated applications of the implications. This is especially true of the last six of the commandments, those that deal directly with man's relationship to his fellow man.

> Almost all laws are derived from the Ten Commandments.

Politics has to do with the way governments and people interact, especially over money and power. Governmental institutions, including our legal systems, are a mix of law and politics. This is partially because of their use of persuasive pressure (and enforceability) of law to influence the actual behavior of others.

American politics was mostly founded on Bible-friendly political principles by creationist patriots (most of whom were Bible-revering Protestants, as the US Supreme Court once admitted). Many judges now view law itself as inherently secular and evolving.

With evolutionary-based politics, no one's basic rights are really secure because political rights once deemed absolute and inalienable (such as a baby's right to be born or a family's right to its homestead unless the property is taken for a truly public purpose) are now treated arbitrarily as if those rights were mere privileges that governments may revoke at will.

To the extent that government officials no longer respect God as the ultimate authority, they functionally substitute their own power for His, using the evolutionary logic that "might makes right" instead of the Bible-friendly rule-of-law logic that right justifies might.

Environment and ecology

In Eden, and again after the flood, God commanded mankind to exercise a steward's dominion over all the earth and its many life forms, land animals, sea animals, birds, and so forth. This is a God-ordained mandate for the whole human race and is in conjunction with God's decree that humans be fruitful and multiply. To obey this mandate, mankind must understand the earth and its inhabitants, weather, and other environmental factors that combine into the interactive whole of the earth's ecology.

Ecology is the study of the ongoing interrelatedness of all of earth's life forms (including humans and the huge variety of animals, plants, bacteria, and so on) with all of the inanimate environmental elements, such as soil, air, and water.

How do fish live in the sea? How do birds fly in the air? How and why do some animals seasonally migrate or hibernate or postpone gestation?

Mankind has God-assigned authority to use, consume, and otherwise manage animals, plants, and the physical environment (such as diverting river water for irrigation, harnessing wind power for sailing and windmills, or using rock for buildings). But this authority is a stewardship that requires rules that promote unselfishness, wise agriculture, and conservation.

Man's dominion (his rule or management) is right only when it accords with God's revealed will for the earth. Moral standards for doing that are found in the Bible.

> Man's dominion (his rule or management) is right only when it accords with God's revealed will for the earth.

Ethics and justice

Ethics and justice should be complementary, ensuring both the moral and legal rightness of mankind's choices and actions. What should be the standard for how we determine right and wrong?

Ethics concerns what is morally right or wrong. Justice concerns what is legally right or wrong. Ideally, justice is ethical, and one assumes that doing what is ethical is legal. Justice cares about people's rights and about righting wrongs when those rights are violated. Although

Cain denied being his brother's keeper, we expect ethical standards and administered justice to function as brothers' keepers (especially when we ourselves are the brothers!).

Justice can be restorative (compensatory), requiring the wrongdoer to restore the innocent victim, to the extent possible, to the same (or a similar) condition the victim was in before the wrong was committed. This might include paying to repair damaged property, paying hospital bills, or returning stolen goods. Or justice can be punitive (penal), punishing criminals for the wrongs they commit as a matter of social morality. This may involve jail time, fines, loss of a driver's license, a criminal record, or even capital punishment.

But sometimes the boundaries of what is morally right (ethical) are controversial. What about cloning, or artificial insemination, or various forms of contraception? What about informing human subjects that they are being experimented on for scientific or marketing research purposes? What about the use of deception by government officials in the name of national security, or to avoid a riot, or to prevent social injustice? What about civil rights, discrimination, and the persecution of Christians?

The Bible provides knowable answers to all of these moral decision-making questions, either directly or indirectly. The Bible's moral values are not like relativistic situational ethics. The Bible provides moral absolutes, such as "thou shalt not steal," "thou shalt not murder," and "as ye would that men should do to you, do ye also to them likewise."

The Long View

> Thus saith the LORD the maker thereof, the LORD that formed it, to establish it; the LORD is his name; call unto me, and I will answer thee, and show thee great and mighty things, which thou knowest not (Jeremiah 33:2-3).

Christians frequently face the challenging problem of time. Human perspective is usually limited to the understanding we gain during our lifetimes with an occasional increased awareness from the study of history. Our confidence rests in the fact that the Lord is the Alpha and Omega and that He knows the end from the beginning. But our prayers and our faith are sorely tested when the answers to the desires of our heart are delayed.

Jeremiah is often referred to as the weeping prophet, primarily because he composed the epic Old Testament poem Lamentations. Jeremiah had been called by God to prophesy to a king and to a nation the fact that God was about to punish them severely for their apostasy. As far as we can tell, no one in authority ever listened to him.

In fact, King Zedekiah of Judah threw Jeremiah into prison and chained him up because the king did not like (or believe) the prophecy that the Lord directly dictated to Jeremiah about the coming war with and subsequent captivity by Nebuchadnezzar.

But the Lord had future plans for Judah. So God told Jeremiah (while he was still in prison) to purchase a piece of land there from his cousin Hanameel because God was going to restore Judah (Jeremiah 32:6-12). Hanameel got all the paperwork together and brought the "evidences" to the prison along with the necessary witnesses, and the deal was struck.

Jeremiah, knowing full well that Judah was going to be sacked and burned by a ruthless army, nonetheless believed the Lord's promise and spent his own money for a piece of property that others would have considered worthless if the nation was about to go under.

Those were the conditions under which Jeremiah understood God's promise, "Call unto me, and I will answer thee, and show thee great and mighty things, which thou knowest not." Had Jeremiah been like most of us, he would have begged for freedom from prison, or the healing of his nation, or the salvation of his jailers. But God had given him the promise that He would punish and then restore the nation—go buy some property for the future!

It is really easy for us to miss God's "long view." We get depressed by economic recessions or caught up in the political unbelief of the world's behavior, and we miss out on the opportunities of God's direction and plans for the future.

Our heavenly Father has plans for you and for me, for our churches, and yes, for the Institute for Creation Research. The general orders are to "occupy" until the Lord returns (Luke 19:13). All of us need to take the long view.

That surely means trying to prepare for the next generation. That surely means seeking first the kingdom of God above all other priorities. That surely means focusing our time, our energy, our plans, and yes, our resources on eternal values rather than the short-term circumstances of a brief life on a dying earth.

May God give us the vision of the "things which are not seen" (2 Corinthians 4:18).

Summarizing the Evidence

Authentic text. Today's Bibles have been translated from sources so reliable that there is no room for any reasonable doubt as to the authenticity of Scripture.

Accurate data. When the Scripture makes comments about prior events, places, science, or even what was once in the future, those comments always match real-world discoveries from history and science.

Assessable results. Application of biblical principles in every human endeavor shows that God's advice is successfully livable, right, and true.

Biblical Insight

1. Compare 2 Peter 3:16 with 2 Timothy 3:16.

   - How did Peter distinguish Paul's writings from other contemporary correspondence?

   - The subsection above titled "Reliable Eyewitnesses" referred to humans and God as coauthors of Scripture. In reviewing the meaning of inspiration from the 2 Timothy passage, describe what role each coauthor took in the process.

   - What features did Peter likely notice in Paul's writings that led him to consider them as Scripture?

2. Genesis 9:1-17 has been called the Noahic covenant. What specific changes, compared to the preflood "world that

then was" (2 Peter 3:6) were instituted at this moment from each of these Noahic covenant statements, and why do you think each change was necessary?

- "The fear of you and the dread of you shall be upon every beast of the earth, and upon every fowl of the air, upon all that moveth upon the earth, and upon all the fishes of the sea; into your hand are they delivered" (verse 2).

- "Every moving thing that liveth shall be meat for you; even as the green herb have I given you all things" (verse 3).

- "Whoso sheddeth man's blood, by man shall his blood be shed: for in the image of God made he man" (verse 6).

- "I will establish my covenant with you, neither shall all flesh be cut off any more by the waters of a flood; neither shall there any more be a flood to destroy the earth" (verse 11).

Part 2

Examining the Incompatibility
of Creation and Evolution

8

Why Recent Creation
Is a Vital Doctrine

A growing number of technically and theologically trained Christians are trying to wed the evolutionary doctrine of naturalistic development with the biblical account of creation recorded in the book of Genesis. Various hybrid theories have waxed and waned over the past 150 years, and unfortunately, all of them have emanated from Christians, not from evolutionists. Naturalistic and atheistic evolutionists are content to ignore and exclude every religious text, especially the Bible.

Some Christians believe it is possible to pick and choose the parts of the Bible they would like to follow and either ignore or deny the rest, but that self-pleasing censorship is certainly not consistent with the message of the Bible. "Every word of God is pure," the Scripture insists. "Add thou not unto his words, lest he reprove thee, and thou be found a liar" (Proverbs 30:5-6).

So why is there confusion surrounding the account of creation in Genesis 1–2? Is there any merit to the so-called scientific claims of millions and billions of years of biological development? Is Scripture ambiguous on the issues related to the origin of life, the entrance of death, or the awful flood of Noah's day? Was the Genesis record simply written as a symbolic framework for later generations to adapt as needed in light of scientific discoveries?

The evidence—both biblical and scientific—suggests otherwise.

A right understanding of the biblical account of creation is especially important for those who trust their eternal destiny to Jesus Christ, the One who proclaims Himself to be the Creator of everything that exists. Common sense dictates that God's revealed Word must be true—or the God of the Bible is a fraud and a liar.

Those of us who still believe not only that the Bible is the inerrant Word of God but also that God intended it to be understood by ordinary people (not just by scholarly specialists in science or theology) have been labeled "young-earth creationists."

We did not choose that name for ourselves. But we believe that God is capable of saying what He means and means what He says, so we have to believe that the whole creation is far younger than evolutionists can accept.

It would be much more comfortable for us *not* to believe in a young earth. The entire scientific and educational establishments are committed to old-earth evolutionism, and so are the supposedly more intellectual segments of the religious world. Many mainline seminaries and colleges have capitulated to theistic evolutionism, and most evangelical colleges and seminaries espouse old-earth creationism, or what many call progressive creationism.

So young-earth creationism is not a comfortable position to hold, especially for scientists or ambitious students, and it would be tempting either to give it up or else just to say it really doesn't matter how or when God created (as do most modern churches and parachurch organizations) as long as we believe that He is our Creator.

But it does matter, and that is why the Institute for Creation Research was formed in the first place more than 40 years ago. Our very statement of faith specifies this position. And it's important to emphasize once again why it is vital to continue to believe, as our Christian forefathers did, that "in six days, the LORD made heaven and earth, the sea, and all that in them is, and rested the seventh day" (Exodus 20:11).

Implications of the Old-Earth Position

Belief in a 4.6 billion-year-old earth and a 15 billion-year-old universe obviously did not come from the Bible, for nowhere in the Bible do we find even a hint of evolution or long geologic ages. Readers who examine every relevant verse in every book of the Bible will not find one suggestion anywhere of the geologic or astronomical ages that are widely assumed today. The concepts of evolution and an infinitely old cosmos are often found in the ancient pagan religions but never in the original Judeo-Christian literature.

Therefore, Christians who want to harmonize the standard geologic/astronomical age system with Scripture must use eisegesis, not exegesis, to do so. That is, they have to try to interpret Scripture in such a way as to make it fit modern scientism. We believe, on the other hand, that the only way we can really honor the Bible as God's inspired Word is to assume it as authoritative on all subjects with which it deals. That means we must use the Bible to interpret scientific data rather than using naturalistic presuppositions to direct our Bible interpretations.

Those who choose the latter course embark on a very slippery slope that ends at a precipice. For if the long geologic ages really took place, then at least a billion years of suffering and death in the animal kingdom transpired before the arrival of men and women in the world. Each geologic age is identified by the types of dead organisms now preserved as fossils in the rocks of that age, and there are literally billions of such fossils buried in the earth's crust. This fact leads to the following very disturbing chain of conclusions.

1. God is not really a God of grace and mercy after all, for He seems to have created a world filled with animals suffering and dying for a billion years, and He did so for no apparent reason whatever, assuming that His ultimate goal was to create human beings for fellowship with Himself.

2. The Bible is not really an authoritative guide, for if it is wrong in these important matters of science and history, which we supposedly can check for ourselves using the usual criteria of scientific and historical investigation, then how can we trust it in matters of salvation, heaven, and everlasting life, which we have no means of verifying scientifically? "If I have told you earthly things, and ye believe not," said Jesus, "how shall ye believe, if I tell you of heavenly things?" (John 3:12).

3. Death is not really the wages of sin, as the Bible says, for violence, pain, and death reigned in the world long before sin came in.

God is directly responsible for this cruel regime, not Adam. Furthermore, when God observed the completed creation of "every thing that he had made...the heavens and the earth...and all the host of them," He pronounced it all to be "very good" (Genesis 1:31; 2:1). This seems to imply that God is sadistic, taking pleasure in observing the suffering and dying of His creatures.

4. The Bible teaches that Jesus Christ was our Creator before He became our Savior (John 1:1-3,10; Colossians 1:16; etc.). But Christ thought that it was "from the beginning of the creation" (not billions of years after the beginning of the creation) that "God made them male and female" (Mark 10:6, referencing Genesis 1:27). If He had really been there at the beginning, He would have known better. Furthermore, if God had really created a world of nature "red in tooth and claw," leading to the survival of the fittest, how could His Son later teach His followers that "whosoever will save his life shall lose it" (Mark 8:35) and tell them, "Love your enemies" and "do good to them that hate you" (Matthew 5:44)?

5. Still more significantly, if physical human death was not really an important part of the penalty for sin, then the agonizingly cruel physical death of Christ on the cross was not necessary to pay that penalty and thus would be a gross miscarriage of justice on God's part.

6. This would lead us to conclude further that we have no real Savior. Christ is no longer here on earth, but sin and death are still here, so the promises in the Bible concerning future salvation seem to have been just empty rhetoric. If God's Word was wrong about creation and about the meaning of Christ's death, its prophecies and promises concerning the future are obviously of no value either.

7. Finally, we have no reason to believe in God at all—at least not in the personal, loving, omniscient, omnipotent, holy, righteous God that the Bible makes Him out to be. If that kind of God really existed, He would never have created the groaning, suffering, dying world implied by the long ages required for evolution. If suffering and death in the world—especially the suffering and death of Christ—are not the result of God's judgment on sin in the world, then the most reasonable inference is that the God of the Bible does not exist. The slippery slope of

compromise finally ends in the dark chasm of atheism, at least for those who travel to its logical termination.

The evolutionary system has been entrenched for so long that many people who otherwise accept the Bible as infallible have deemed it expedient to compromise on this issue. Thus, evolution has been called "God's method of creation," and the Genesis record of the six days of creation has been reinterpreted in terms of the evolutionary ages of historical geology. These geologic ages have either been placed in an assumed gap between Genesis 1:1 and 1:2 or identified with the days of creation.

Theories of this kind raise more problems than they solve, however. It is more productive to take the Bible literally and then to interpret the actual facts of science within its revelatory framework. If the Bible cannot be understood, it is useless as revelation. If it contains scientific fallacies, it could not have been given by inspiration.

All the theories described below seek to accommodate the Bible to evolutionary geology. They are biblically and scientifically invalid and should be abandoned.

Theistic Evolution

Evolution is believed by its leading advocates to be a basic principle of continual development, of increasing order and complexity throughout the universe. In this line of thinking, the complex elements developed from simpler elements, living organisms evolved from non-living chemicals, complex forms of life evolved from simpler organisms, and even man himself gradually evolved from some kind of apelike ancestor. Religions, cultures, and other social institutions are likewise continually evolving into higher forms.

Thus, evolution is a complete worldview, an explanation of origins and meanings without the necessity of a personal God who created and upholds all things. This philosophy is so widely and persuasively taught in our schools, Christians are often tempted to accept the compromise position of theistic evolution, according to which evolution is viewed as God's method of creation. However, this is an inconsistent and contradictory position. Here are three reasons why.

1. It contradicts the biblical record of creation. The first chapter of Genesis tells us ten times that God created plants and animals to reproduce "after their kinds." The biblical word *kind* may be broader than our modern word *species*, but at least it implies definite limits to variation. The New Testament writers accepted the full historicity of the Genesis account of creation. Even Christ Himself quoted from it as historically accurate and authoritative (Matthew 19:4-6).

2. It is inconsistent with God's methods. The standard concept of evolution involves the development of innumerable misfits and extinctions, useless and even harmful organisms. If this is God's method of creation, it is strange that He would use such cruel, haphazard, inefficient, wasteful processes. Furthermore, the idea of the survival of the fittest, the idea that the stronger animals eliminate the weaker in the struggle for existence, is the essence of Darwin's theory of evolution by natural selection. But this whole scheme is flatly contradicted by the biblical doctrine of love, of unselfish sacrifice, and of Christian charity. The God of the Bible is a God of order and of grace, not a God of confusion and cruelty.

3. The evolutionary philosophy is the intellectual basis of all antitheistic systems. It served Hitler as the rationale for Nazism and Marx as the supposed scientific basis for communism. It is the basis of the various modern methods of psychology and sociology that treat man merely as a higher animal and that have led to the misnamed "new morality" and ethical relativism. It has provided the pseudoscientific rationale for racism and military aggression. Its whole effect on the world and mankind has been harmful and degrading. Jesus said, "A good tree cannot bring forth evil fruit" (Matthew 7:18). The evil fruit of the evolutionary philosophy is evidence enough of its evil roots.

Thus, evolution is biblically unsound, theologically contradictory, and sociologically harmful.

Progressive Creation

Some Christians use the term *progressive creation* instead of *theistic evolution*, the difference being the suggestion that God interjected occasional acts of creation at critical points throughout the geologic ages. Thus, for example, man's soul was created even though his body evolved from an apelike ancestor.

This concept is even less acceptable than theistic evolution, however. It charges God with not only waste and cruelty (through its commitment to the geologic ages) but also ignorance and incompetence. God's postulated intermittent creative efforts show either that He didn't know what He wanted when He started the process or that He couldn't provide it with enough energy to sustain it until it reached its goal. A god who would have to create man by any such cut-and-try, discontinuous, injurious method as this can hardly be the omniscient, omnipotent, loving God of the Bible.

The Day-Age Theory

According to the established system of historical geology, the history of the earth is divided into a number of geologic ages. The earth and its inhabitants are supposed to have evolved into their present form during a vast span of geologic ages beginning about a billion years ago.

In contrast, the biblical revelation tells us that God created the entire universe in six days only a few thousand years ago. Consequently, many Christian scholars have tried to find some way of reinterpreting Genesis to fit the framework of history prescribed by geologists.

The most popular of these devices has been the day-age theory, by which the days of creation are interpreted figuratively as the ages of geology. However, this theory has many serious difficulties.

The Hebrew word for *day* is *yom*, and the word can occasionally be used to mean an indefinite period of time if the context warrants. In the overwhelming preponderance of its occurrences in the Old Testament, however, it means a literal day—that is, either an entire solar day or the daylight portion of a solar day. It was, in fact, defined by God Himself the very first time it was used, in Genesis 1:5, where we are told that "God called the light Day." It thus means, in the context, the day in the succession of day and night, or light and darkness.

Furthermore, the word always refers to a solar day when it is used in a succession of similar periods (that is, "the first day," "the second day," and so on) or with definite terminal points (such as "evening and morning"). And it is used this way hundreds of times in the Bible.

Still further, the plural form of the word (Hebrew, *yamim*) is used more than 700 times in the Old Testament and always, without exception, refers to literal days. A statement in the Ten Commandments written on a tablet of stone directly by God Himself is very significant in this connection, for He uses this word and says plainly, "In six days, the LORD made heaven and earth, the sea, and all that in them is" (Exodus 20:11).

The day-age theory is not only unacceptable scripturally but also impossible to reconcile with the geologic position with which it attempts to compromise. There are more than 20 serious contradictions between the biblical order and events of the creative days and the standard geologic history of the earth and its development even if the days are interpreted as ages. For example, the Bible teaches that the earth existed before the stars, that it was initially covered by water, that fruit trees appeared before fishes, that plant life preceded the sun, that the first animals created were the whales, that birds were made before insects, that man was created before woman, and many other such things, all of which are contradicted by historical geologists and paleontologists.

But the most serious fallacy in the day-age theory is theological. It makes God directly responsible for five billion years of purposeless variation, accidental changes, evolutionary blind alleys, numerous misfits and extinctions, cruel struggles for existence, preservation of the strong and extermination of the weak, natural disasters of all kinds, rampant disease, disorder, decay, and above all, death. The Bible teaches that at the end of the creation period, God pronounced His whole creation to be very good in spite of all this. It also teaches plainly that this world's present groaning and travailing in pain (Romans 8:22) resulted from man's sin and God's curse. "By one man sin entered into the world, and death by sin" (Romans 5:12). "God is not the author of confusion" (1 Corinthians 14:33).

The Gap Theory

Another attempt to harmonize the first chapter of Genesis with the geologic ages has been to place them into an imaginary "gap" between Genesis 1:1 and 1:2. In this scenario, the original world God created existed for millions or perhaps billions of years before being destroyed in a global cataclysm that left it void. God then re-created the world we see now. In essence, God started over, wiping out all of earth's previous creatures, who bear no genetic connection to earth's current life forms. Proponents believe this allows them to accept both the old earth of evolutionary theory and the literal creation depicted in Genesis.

But like the day-age theory, the gap theory involves numerous serious fallacies. A catastrophe that wiped out all life and left the earth empty and underwater would have been powerful enough to destroy fossil-bearing strata.

The geologic ages cannot be disposed of merely by ignoring the extensive fossil record on which they are based. These supposed ages are inextricably involved in the entire structure of the evolutionary history of the earth and its inhabitants, including man. The fossil record is the best evidence for evolution (in fact, the only such evidence that indicates evolution on more than a trivial scale). Furthermore, the geologic ages are recognized and identified specifically by the fossil contents of the sedimentary rocks in the earth's crust. The very names of the ages show this. Thus, the Paleozoic era is the era of ancient life, the Mesozoic era is the era of intermediate life, and the Cenozoic era is the era of recent life. At a matter of fact, the one primary means for dating these rocks in the first place has always been the supposed "stage of evolution" of the fossils they contain.

Thus, acceptance of the geologic ages implicitly involves acceptance of the whole evolutionary package. Most of the fossil forms preserved in the sedimentary rocks have obvious relatives in the present world, so the gap theory includes a "re-creation" scheme in which the Creator re-creates in six days the same animals and plants that had been previously developed slowly over long ages, only to perish violently in a great pre-Adamic cataclysm.

The gap theory, therefore, really does not face the evolution issue at all, but merely pigeonholes it in an imaginary gap between Genesis 1:1 and 1:2. It leaves unanswered the serious problem as to why God would use the method of slow evolution over long ages in the primeval world, then destroy it, and then use the method of special creation to re-create the same forms He had just destroyed.

Furthermore, there is no geologic evidence of such a worldwide cataclysm in recent geologic history. In fact, the very concept of a worldwide cataclysm precludes the geologic ages, which are based specifically on the assumption that there have been no such worldwide cataclysms. As a device for harmonizing Genesis with geology, the gap theory is self-defeating.

The greatest problem with the theory is that it makes God the direct author of evil. It implies that He used the methods of struggle, violence, decay, and death on a worldwide scale for at least three billion years in order to accomplish His unknown purposes in the primeval world. This is the testimony of the fossils and the geologic ages that the theory tries to place before Genesis 1:2. Then, according to the theory, Satan sinned against God in heaven (Isaiah 14:12-15; Ezekiel 28:11-17), and God cast him out of heaven to the earth, destroying the earth in the process in the supposed pre-Adamic cataclysm. Satan's sin in heaven, however, cannot in any way account for the agelong spectacle of suffering and death in the world during the geologic ages that preceded his sin! Thus, God alone remains responsible for suffering, death, and confusion—without any reason for it.

The Scripture says, on the other hand, at the end of the six days of creation, "God saw everything that he had made [including not only the entire earth and all its contents, but all the heavens as well—note Genesis 1:16; 2:2], and, behold, it was very good" (Genesis 1:31). Death did not enter the world until man sinned (Romans 5:12; 1 Corinthians 15:21). Evidently even Satan's rebellion in heaven had not yet taken place, because everything was pronounced "very good" there too.

The real answer to the meaning of the great terrestrial graveyard—the fossil contents of the great beds of hardened sediments all over the world—will be found neither in the slow operation of uniform natural processes over vast ages of time nor in an imaginary cataclysm that took place before the six days of God's perfect creation. Rather, it will be found in a careful study of the very real worldwide cataclysm described in Genesis 6–9 and confirmed in many other parts of the Bible and in the early records of nations and tribes all over the world, namely, the great flood of the days of Noah.

These four evolutionary theories, which attempt to harmonize the Bible with evolution, have shown that such a task is impossible to do legitimately. We must conclude, therefore, that if the Bible is really the Word of God (as its writers allege and as we believe), then evolution and its geologic age system must be completely false. The Bible cannot be reinterpreted to correlate with evolution, so Christians must diligently proceed to correlate the facts of science with the Bible.

Where We Must Stand

Therefore, regardless of how much more convenient it would be to adopt the old-earth approach or to believe the issue doesn't matter, we cannot. The Bible is the inerrant, infallible, inspired Word of the living, gracious, omnipotent Creator; the Lord Jesus Christ is our crucified and risen Savior; and all the real facts of science and history support these truths.

On the other hand, there is no genuine scientific evidence for evolutionism. No true evolution from one kind of organism to a more complex kind has been observed in all human history, and there is no recorded history beyond the approximately 6000 years of biblical history. Any alleged earlier ages have to be postulated on the discredited assumption of uniformitarianism. If such imaginary ages ever existed, why did they leave no credible fossil records of real evolutionary transitions among the billions of fossils preserved in the rocks?

What the fossils *do* show is death—rapid death and burial, in fact, or they would not have been preserved at all. And death speaks of sin and judgment, not evolution and long ages. Pain and death are not good things, and a loving God would not call them good. They are instead "the wages of sin" (Romans 6:23). This judgment by our all-holy Creator necessarily fell on Adam, his descendants, and the dominion over which God had placed him.

In the new earth, which God in Christ will create after sin is finally purged out of this groaning creation, however, "there shall be no more death, neither sorrow, nor crying, neither shall there be any more pain" (Revelation 21:4). Once again, God's creation will all be very good!

In the meantime, we do well to continue to believe His Word just as it stands. God forbid that we should ever be like those who "loved the praise of men more than the praise of God" (John 12:43).

Summarizing the Evidence

Science and the Bible. The proper understanding of science will always lead to a confirmation of the biblical text.

Old-earth thinking. Evolutionary and hybrid theories of creation denigrate both the character of God and the integrity of Scripture.

Recent creation. The facts of science and the Bible, rightly interpreted, affirm the existence of a young earth.

Biblical Insight

Read the creation accounts in Genesis 1–2.

1. What indicators does God use in these verses that invalidate theistic evolution?

2. Consider the timing of creation in relation to the fall. Does the text anywhere indicate that death occurred before the fall?

3. Write down any patterns you see in the order of creation and God's response each day.

9

The Bible Does Not Allow an Evolutionary Interpretation

The biblical account of creation is not restricted only to the book of Genesis. References to creation are made throughout the Bible except in the one-chapter personal epistles of Paul, John, and Jude (Philemon; 2–3 John; Jude). Many of the great promises of God are based on the evidence of His creative power and work. The creation is not merely an allegorical story intended for moral instruction; it is treated throughout the rest of the Bible as a historical occurrence and is specifically documented as such.

In the New Testament Gospels, the Lord Jesus alluded to the early chapters of Genesis no fewer than 25 times. Other New Testament writers cite or refer to them another 175 times. In each instance, the events are cited as real history rather than allegory or metaphor from which we might simply derive a spiritual meaning. Either Jesus ("the way, the truth, and the life"—John 14:6) was speaking truth, or He was deluded—or worse yet, He was lying to accommodate the supposed scientific ignorance of the day.

No Hint of Evolutionary Development

No human was around to observe the origin of the universe, so we must all begin with presuppositional belief. Either God's Word is true about the creation or modern scientific theory is true about the ages-long evolutionary development of all things through random processes. They cannot both be true. They are mutually exclusive.

Let there be no doubt. The Bible contains no reference, no inference, no metaphorical allegory, no hint of evolutionary development from simple to more complex life forms by blind, random chance. Nature, Psalm 19:1-3 boldly insists, has "speech" and "knowledge" that every day and every night declare the glory of God. "The creation," Paul affirms in Romans 1:20, manifests even the "invisible things" of God so that they are "clearly seen" in the physical and visible universe that He has created. Design, order, purpose, promises, goals, prophecy—all are written into the worlds that God has made. Nowhere does Scripture give credence to an evolutionary theory of origins.

> Nowhere does Scripture give credence to an evolutionary theory of origins.

Genesis 1:1–2:4 details the creation account carefully and thoroughly, day by day. So precise is the language that it appears that God carefully chose both the terms and the grammar to ensure that we could not mistake their meanings. God even makes a distinction between "creating" (bringing something into existence where nothing existed before), and "making" and "shaping" that which was created. God spoke, and it was done (Psalm 33:9). God commanded, and the great host of heaven was created (Psalm 148:5).

Anytime man attempts to discover *how* God created, using his natural mind and his present ability to test and verify the processes of nature, he is doomed to failure. The Bible declares that "the worlds were framed by the word of God, so that things which are seen were not made of things which do appear" (Hebrews 11:3). Science is limited to what can be observed as well as by the finite intellect with which man reasons, attempts to theorize, devises various tests, and tries to describe omnipotence.

Evolution is a story invented by man in order to exclude God from his life. Others have adapted it and tried to force an interpretation of Genesis in which God allegedly uses mechanistic and naturalistic processes to create. Modern man is really good at telling the story of evolution! But that is *not* what the Bible says or teaches. Not even close.

The Gospel of John begins by specifically identifying Jesus Christ as the Creator of all things (John 1:1-3). Paul confirms this in greater detail in Colossians 1:15-16.

> [God's dear Son] is the image of the invisible God, the first-born of every creature: for by him were all things created, that are in heaven, and that are in earth, visible and invisible, whether they be thrones, or dominions, or principalities, or powers: all things were created by him, and for him.

Christ alone—not natural laws or evolutionary processes—is worthy "to receive glory and honor and power," because Christ alone created all things (Revelation 4:11). His careful omniscient and omnipotent work could never be attributed to evolutionary processes and still conform to the truth given in the biblical record.

The simple fact is that God had no need to use evolutionary ages in His creation. The omnipotent and omniscient power of the Creator is the basis for all our trust in God. Anyone who reads the obvious attributes of God identified in the pages of Scripture cannot deny that God is capable of creating the universe in six days. There is no reason to diminish the work of God by attributing it to time and chance, and less reason to doubt His written words. The creation did not come into being through billions of years of natural processes. With merely a word, all was accomplished, to last in its wholeness forever (Psalm 148:3-6).

> There is no reason to diminish the work of God by attributing it to time and chance.

Faith, which all thinking beings must have to exist in our universe, can either be foolish (believing the moon is made out of green cheese, for example) or, as the Bible defines it, "the substance of things hoped for, the evidence of things not seen" (Hebrews 11:1). Science places an enormous amount of faith in the promise that God Himself made in Genesis 8:22: "While the earth remaineth, seedtime and harvest, and cold and heat, and summer and winter, and day and night shall not cease."

Science, even evolutionary science, bases its theories, its predictions, and its conclusions on the stability of physical laws. Evolutionary science makes the mistake of extending the promise of God for stability in this world backward to the processes of creation at the beginning of the world.

Living faith in God begins with faith in His work as Creator (Hebrews 11:3). What exists in the world today was not crafted or developed from preexisting material. It was made specifically and instantaneously from nothing by the omnipotent and omniscient special creation of God.

The Bible uses precise language about the duration of creation.

The very concept of a day is defined explicitly in the first chapter of Genesis: "God called the light Day, and the darkness he called Night. And the evening and the morning were the first day" (Genesis 1:5).

Just as we measure time by days, which are defined by the passage of the sun, so God originally measured time as the darkness passing into light. That first night-day cycle was called day one. The same formula is repeated for each of the six days of God's initial workweek. Once again, God seems to go out of His way to make sure that we could not mistake what He meant. Surely God used the clearest possible way to define the time involved.

Later, with His own finger, God wrote on the stone tablets of the Ten Commandments, "Six days shalt thou labor, and do all thy work: but the seventh day is the sabbath of the LORD...for in six days the LORD made heaven and earth, the sea, and all that in them is, and rested on the seventh day" (Exodus 20:9-11). This comparison between the six days of labor that all men experience and the seven days of the creation cannot possibly be taken as an allegorical allusion to immeasurable eons.

The only reason Scripture provides for why God did not create the entire universe in a single day is that God intended the creation week to be a template so man would know how to best function with the life God had created. God, who needs no rest for Himself, in His compassion anticipated and planned for man's rest. Jesus gave the reason: "The sabbath was made for man, and not man for the sabbath" (Mark 2:27).

This regular day that God established in the creation week is denoted in Hebrew by the word *yom* (plural *yamim*). That word is used more than 3000 times in the Old Testament. In Genesis 1:5, it is precisely delineated as the passing of darkness into light, or one solar day. It is coupled with the expression "the evening and the morning" 38 times and is accompanied by a numerical modifier 359 times (that is, "the eighth day," "the seventeenth day," and so on). The plural form appears 845 times. In none of these 1242 references can the word mean anything other than a literal, 24-hour, solar day. The context is absolutely clear.

The rest of the 1758 times the Hebrew word *yom* appears in its singular form are *never* used to speak of an eon-long age. Occasionally, *day* may be used to identify an unspecified period of time, as in the "day of trouble" (Psalm 20:1) or the "day of the Lord" (used 24 times in the Old Testament) or, as is in the case of Genesis 2:4, "in the day that the Lord God made the earth and the heavens." The only reason to translate *day* as *age* is to accommodate the required eons of evolution. Evolutionary thinking must have long, inexplicable, unthinkable ages to work and cannot accept the literal six-day creation that is recorded in Genesis.

> The only reason to translate *day* as *age* is to accommodate the required eons of evolution.

The first verse is God's first test of faith.

Some have suggested that God set down a "faith test" with this very first of His words to His creation. Obviously, Genesis 1:1 is unique among all the hundreds of sacred books of the various religions of the world. With those words, we are confronted with the simple question, do we believe what God says?

This first verse of the Bible refutes all of man's false philosophies about origins and the meaning of the world.

- It repudiates atheism because the universe was created by God.

- It repudiates pantheism because God transcends all He created.

- It repudiates polytheism because only one God created all things.

- It repudiates materialism because matter had a beginning.

- It repudiates dualism because God was alone when He created.

- It repudiates humanism because God, not man, is the ultimate reality.

- It repudiates evolutionism because God created all things.

The creation account does not match evolutionary progression.

The biblical record is not at all compatible with the story of evolution. Several foundational premises are in conflict with each other. Some hybrid theories of what could be called *crevolution*—devised by Christians—insist that the creation account in Scripture describes an order of development that is essentially the same as the order of evolutionary development. That is simply not so.

Those who propose such nonsense are either ignorant of what is recorded in Genesis, or they deliberately preach falsehood to make their particular brand of hybrid compromise fit the atheistic story of evolutionary science. Even a quick glance at the Genesis record manifests irresolvable conflicts, as the table on the next page shows.

Perhaps one could say that the account in Genesis shows a progression from simple to complex, but it is absolutely out of sequence with evolutionary theory. The specific information in Genesis agrees perfectly with the many other passages in the Bible that speak of the creation week, and it is so obviously different from the order of evolutionary development that one wonders why there is even an attempt to reconcile the two. Evolutionists will never accept these hybrid theories.

The Order of Creation	The Story of Evolution
Matter was created by God.	Matter has existed forever.
Earth was created before the sun and stars.	The sun and stars existed before the earth.
The ocean was formed before land.	Land existed before the ocean.
Light was created before the sun.	The sun was the earth's first light.
Land plants were earth's first life.	Marine organisms were earth's first life.
Plants were created before the sun.	The sun existed long before plants.
Fruit trees were created before fish.	Fish existed long before fruit trees.
Birds were created before insects.	Insects existed long before birds.
Birds were created before reptiles.	Reptiles existed before birds.
Man lived before there was rain.	Rain fell before man existed.
Man was created before the woman.	A female *Homo sapiens* developed first.
Man was uniquely formed in perfection.	Man took ages to develop from apes.
The creation is completed.	Evolutionary development is ongoing.

Evolution requires an unbiblical role of death.

One final thought. Evolution depends on death. Death, for the evolutionist, is a good process that weeds out the unfit, making possible the survival of the fittest. Without the death of countless billions of life forms over eons of unrecorded time, evolution could not occur. For the evolutionist, therefore, death and time are absolute necessities—the key elements that make the process possible.

On the other hand, the biblical record introduces death as a judgment, the Creator's curse on the fallen creation (Genesis 3:17-19). Death is an intrusion into that which God had pronounced "very good" when He evaluated His week of creative activity on the sixth day. The Bible identifies death as the last enemy (1 Corinthians 15:26), which will be destroyed by the Creator in the new heaven and new earth (Revelation 21:1,4). According to the biblical record, death did not enter the world until Adam, the steward and co-regent given responsibility for the care of the creation, dared to rebel against his Creator and was sentenced and banned from the garden in Eden (Romans 5:12).

These many and obvious conflicts between the historical record of creation in Scripture and the evolutionary story of origins ought to settle the issue for Christians—certainly for those who believe that the Bible is God's holy Word. The Bible is clear, precise, and comprehensive in its presentation of the evidence for creation. That should be enough even if science disagrees.

> The Bible is clear, precise, and comprehensive in its presentation of the evidence for creation.

Summarizing the Evidence

Evolution and the Bible. The Bible contains no reference or indicator that life developed from the simple to the complex or did so randomly.

Six days. The biblical language confirms that each of the creation days lasted 24 hours.

In the beginning. The very first verse in the Bible confronts us with a Creator who must also be a sovereign Ruler and therefore our Judge.

Biblical Insight

Read Genesis 1 and note the order of God's creative acts.

1. Does the order of creation suggest an evolutionary progression?

2. Do the objects of creation indicate any real transitions from lower forms to higher forms of life?

3. What distinctive characteristics are seen in the creation of man?

10

Science Does Not Observe Evolution
Happening Today

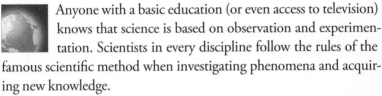Anyone with a basic education (or even access to television) knows that science is based on observation and experimentation. Scientists in every discipline follow the rules of the famous scientific method when investigating phenomena and acquiring new knowledge.

Simply put, a hypothesis (that is, an educated guess) is formed, based on observation or a prediction, and then it is tested and the results are analyzed. If the test results repeatedly verify what the hypothesis anticipated, the scientific method is said to have proven the theory.

Experimental Science

In the pure sciences (physics, chemistry, biology, and so on), evidence must be observable and measurable, and the experiment itself must be repeatable. In the applied sciences (engineering, medicine, pharmacology, and the like), the testing is more rigorous because unknown information may cause the kind of failure that will do great damage. Many scientists insist that to be satisfactorily proven, the hypothesis must be *falsifiable* as well. That standard—which, by the way, is demanded in courts of law whenever scientific evidence is used in a case—simply means that one must understand the processes and procedures used in the testing of the theory so well that the wrong answer must be also known. The scientist must understand the information so thoroughly that he would know what would disprove his theory. This level of rigor is applied by most experimental scientists today.

Adaptive or directed change is not evolution.

Although many experiments have attempted to duplicate some form of evolutionary change (such as from a lower form of life to a higher form or from a mixture of chemicals to some kind of reproducing life form), no one has ever come close to evolving anything in the laboratory. Certain kinds of change can be replicated, such as mutations, which have often produced hideous results in various creatures. But the most brilliant scientists using the most expensive and advanced equipment cannot transform a lower form of life into a higher form.

And yet evolutionary scientists and philosophers strongly believe this to be possible. They insist that because we can see adaptive (horizontal) change among living things (such as big dogs and little dogs), there must be evolutionary (vertical) change among living things over long periods of time (such as some common ancestor developing into both dogs and cats).

Nothing like that is observed in the present.

Scientists have, through selective breeding, made some pretty severe changes to the shapes and sizes of animals. For instance, there are more than 450 breeds of dogs—everything from a tiny Chihuahua to the enormous Great Dane and wolfhound. But they are still dogs. Never has one of these dogs changed into a horse or a pig. The same can be said for cats. Although the Cat Fanciers' Association recognizes 39 breeds of cats, all of the various sizes, shapes, and colors are still cats.

Change among kinds of creatures can happen with or without human intervention, but those changes always remain within very specific and defined limits. No one has witnessed a change from one kind of animal to another.

Evolutionary theory insists that sometime in the unobserved past, a common ancestor to both dogs and cats (possibly a small, meat-eating animal called a *creodont*) began to evolve over time into the different kinds of animals that we now recognize as dogs and cats. However, there is no evidence for such changes—not in the present, certainly, and not in the fossil record. There are no "cogs" or "dats" anywhere! Finches may display variations in beak sizes in isolated population groups (as in Darwin's Galapagos Islands). However, finches do not become woodpeckers. Nor do fish become amphibians. There are no "fincheckers" or "fishibians." Modern science observes absolutely no upward evolution taking place today.

> Modern science observes absolutely no
> upward evolution taking place today.

Natural selection or engineered adaptation?

Natural selection is the process whereby natural environments tend to cull the least fit from some populations. However, nature is unintelligent and is thus unable to choose or select anything. Selection involves intelligence. Rather, created kinds adapt to various environments because they are engineered to adapt. They are programmed by God to fill the earth.

Mutations to the DNA, on the other hand, do change the genetic information. Mutations disrupt the code and cause changes to the life-building process. Most mutations are accidents in the vast and highly complex information instructions of the genome. And most mutations are so small that their effect is unremarkable. Those mutations that impact the genetic information enough to make an observable change are overwhelmingly negative, not beneficial. The unusual creatures that do reach live birth with these observable mutations either die before maturity or are ignored by the rest of the population and do not reproduce.

No one has observed an evolutionary process of upward change taking place today. It does not happen. Evolutionists falsely reason that the evidence of small changes (horizontal) implies the possibility of big changes (vertical) over time. This may appear to be a logical supposition, but it is not observation, and it is definitely not fact.

Summarizing the Evidence

Doing good science. The scientific method depends on observation and experimentation, not speculation.

Natural selection or engineered adaptation. Nature is unintelligent and powerless to select anything, but God programmed within every creature the capacity to adapt to different environments.

Biblical Insight

Compare the creation of the animals and man in Genesis 1 with the work God gave Adam to manage and keep and even name the animals.

1. What reason would God have for establishing the order between man and animals?

2. If animals were ancestors to humans, what does that mean for the mandate God gave to Adam in Genesis 1:28?

3. What evidence of special creation is seen in the creation of Eve?

11

There Is No Evidence Evolution
Took Place in the Past

 No experiment could verify or falsify theories about processes that take place over eons of time, so researchers must turn to historical science for answers.

Historical Science

Historical science, including forensic science, observes clues in the present that may be applied to a possible cause in the past. Archaeologists and paleontologists study origins just as detectives study a murder case. Both practice historical science, which uses present technical information and skills to piece together the remains of a past event or sequence of events.

The archaeologist tries to determine what a past culture, city, or person may have looked like using the various remnants that are uncovered from that period of time. The paleontologist does essentially the same thing but is looking at fossilized bones for clues to what a creature looked like and when and how it lived.

To develop theories about the life forms of the ancient past, paleontologists turn to the fossil record. Almost all prehistoric evidence is contained in the fossil record. And almost all fossils are contained in various types of water-deposited rock. (The rare exceptions are found in amber, peat, and so on). This sedimentary rock was distributed and laid down by water. And that water-deposited rock is all over the planet—even at the tops of mountains.

To demonstrate that simple life forms have changed into more complex life forms over time, evolutionary scientists must produce examples of such changes, often referred to as transitional forms. If indeed the changes occurred slowly over billions of years through mutational accidents, many transitional remains should be available for scientists to uncover and observe in the fossil record.

And the fossil record ought to provide an easily observed progressive order. That is, the deepest level of the water-deposited rock layers (supposedly the most ancient deposits) should contain very simple life forms, such as algae and other single-cell organisms. Further up in the layers (and supposedly nearer to our time), we should find more complex marine invertebrate creatures along with plenty of evidence of the transitional forms that changed from one-cell life to increasingly complex ocean life. Those creatures should have evolved into fish (and they should be found higher up in the water-deposited rock layers), and fish into amphibians, amphibians into reptiles, and so on.

The fossil record supports creation, not evolution.

That's what the evolutionary theory predicted would be found in the fossil record of our ancient past. However, the reality is far from what was expected.

Ninety-five percent of all fossils are marine invertebrates. These highly complex creatures (trilobites, starfish, coral, sponges, jellyfish, clams, ammonites, and more) are found on the tops of mountains, in the middle of deserts, on all land masses on the earth, and in every layer of the various evolutionary eras. The so-called geologic column is full of these marine invertebrates. These fossils are so abundant that evolutionists have named the era the *Cambrian explosion*. The organisms all appear fully formed with absolutely no hint that they evolved from anything else. This layer of first life seems to explode in the fossil record with no incontrovertible observable history prior to the creatures' existence.

That is a real problem for an evolutionary scientist. But it's exactly what would be expected by one who believes the information found in the Bible.

Of the remaining 5 percent of all fossils, 95 percent are plant fossils, typically part of coal beds and seams found everywhere on earth, including the well-known mountain ranges. These coal beds are even found in Antarctica. Ninety-five percent of what is left is comprised mostly of insect fossils (about .02 percent of the whole). And only about .01 percent of all fossils are the so-called "higher order" fossils. This provides very little evidence to work with, and many of these remains are merely pieces of fossilized bone or are so jumbled together that it is almost impossible to tell which bone goes to which creature. Scientists have very little historical evidence to work with when trying to reconstruct the later life forms.

The animals that do exist as complete fossils (mostly marine creatures) are fully formed. The rare larger animals like the dinosaurs and extinct mammals are, in most cases, fragmented or crushed and broken so much that it is very difficult to tell what they really looked like. But in no case is there evidence for transitional forms—other than the fanciful stories invented by theorists and artists for museums and *National Geographic* specials.

Some fossilized creatures once thought to be extinct for millions of years are still in existence today. The best-known example is a fish called the *coelacanth*. In fact, a profusion of such living fossils exist in exactly the same form as in the fossil record.[1] In addition, many life forms that are alive and prospering have ancestors in the fossil record in essentially the same shape and size as we know them (these include the crocodile, the turtle, the bat, many fish, and many insects). None of these has transitioned into anything else over the supposed millions of years of their existence, and no fossil evidence (alive, extinct, or unique) shows the slightest hint of them becoming another kind of creature.

Of course, speculation abounds about how they could have done this or that or how the unusual features of some fossil might have developed into a leg or a wing or experienced some other enormous structural change. But there is no evidence of such change. There is no observed transitional form. What certainly exists in huge quantities is faith—faith in a worldview of unobservable evolutionary development that excludes any supernatural intervention or direction of natural processes.

Evolution requires faith.

Faith in an evolutionary worldview, however, does not depend on evidence. The theory of evolution is a means to an end. The purpose of a naturalistic or mechanistic cosmogony is to provide an atheistic explanation for the existence of all things. Repeatedly in the scientific literature, proponents of evolution insist that neither God nor any other supernatural being can exist. Materialism alone solves the needs of the soul.

> The purpose of a naturalistic or mechanistic cosmogony is to provide an atheistic explanation for the existence of all things.

Harvard professor Richard Lewontin, a geneticist, biologist, and social commentator, wrote an article published in *The New York Review of Books* some years ago that explained why he and his peers were so committed to an atheistic and materialistic worldview:

> Our willingness to accept scientific claims that are against common sense is the key to an understanding of the real struggle between science and the supernatural. We take the side of science in spite of its failure to fulfill many of its extravagant promises of health and life, in spite of the tolerance of the scientific community for just-so stories, because we have a prior commitment to materialism.
>
> It is not that the methods and institutions of science somehow compel us to accept a material explanation of the phenomenal world, but, on the contrary, that we are forced by our a priori adherence to material causes to create an apparatus of investigation and a set of concepts that produce material explanations, no matter how counter-intuitive, no matter how mystifying to the uninitiated. Moreover that materialism is absolute for we cannot allow a Divine foot in the door.[2]

The story of evolution does not have the scientific evidence to support its assertions. It does possess, however, an unyielding resolve to erase God's authority over creation.

Summarizing the Evidence

Forensic science. Forensic science can speculate about the origins of earth, but it cannot replicate.

Digging up fossils. The fossil record is a testimony to rapid burial of creatures caught up in a catastrophic global flood.

Biblical Insight

Read 1 Corinthians 1.

1. How is the wisdom of man described?

2. What is God's reaction to the lofty thoughts of men?

3. How would you apply 1 Corinthians 1 in light of the modern scientific establishment?

12

God's Character Precludes Evolutionary Methods

Everything God has created reveals His eternal power and triune nature so that man has no excuse for not recognizing Him as Creator. "The invisible things of him from the creation of the world are clearly seen, being understood by the things that are made, even his eternal power and Godhead; so that they are without excuse" (Romans 1:20).

Our universe is so vast that man has so far been unable to observe the boundaries of space. The reservoirs of power that can be observed are so huge that we cannot possibly understand how or why they came into being. Educated guesses abound (some of them pretty complex and fanciful—like the Big Bang), but all one can really *know* is that the power seems both eternal and infinite.

Time itself is a great mystery. Its existence is unquestioned, and careful attention is given to its passing. Man uses time and functions within it, but no one really understands what time is, how it came to be, or how to control it. What can be understood is that everything that exists, exists *in* space and *through* time. Even the matter seen and experienced every day consists of various forms of energy in motion during time that produce specific phenomena, such as molecules, trees, planets, and people.

A Universe of Space, Matter, and Time

The universe is both *uni* (one) and *verse* (different). And while something of the three different manifestations of reality (space, matter, and time) can be understood, they cannot be separated from the unit.

Space is invisible and empty, but it is obviously not nothing. No one knows just what it is. Matter is similarly indefinable. Atoms can be split into small pieces, but not even the most gifted scientist can make an atom. In fact, one of the most universal laws of man's reality is that matter can neither be created nor destroyed. The universe could not have created itself.

Man's understanding about the way the universe functions is both simple and profound. Space is the omnipresent background and source of all reality. Everything that exists both resides in space and occupies space. Only when matter moving in and through time produces a phenomenon (an event) does space become evident, allowing man to observe the various things that exist in space (galaxies, stars, planets, trees, people, and so on). Space can be seen only when matter is present.

But to experience anything, time is essential. Matter itself is an ongoing manifestation of complex energies functioning in a specific manner during time. A lifetime is just that: life functioning in and through time. For instance, if I wish to experience my wife (give her a hug or a good-morning kiss), I must use time to cross the space to where her particular form of matter exists and reduce the space that separates us so that we can actually make contact with each other.

God's Signature in the Heavens

Why labor through all of this difficult explanation about space and matter and time? What bearing does this have on the character of God and the impossibility of evolutionary methods? Just this: The Bible clearly states that the created things provide a "clearly seen" illustration of the power and divine nature of the Creator. The universe becomes the "speech" and "language" of God that reveal Him to all humanity (Psalm 19:1-4). God's creation is a picture of what He is like.

God the Father is the invisible, omnipresent background and source of all things. He is transcendent beyond the creation, yet He is ever-present and everywhere present, as the Bible describes: "Whither shall I go from thy spirit? or whither shall I flee from thy presence? If I ascend up into heaven, thou art there: if I make my bed in hell, behold, thou art there" (Psalm 139:7-8).

But the invisible God became visible in the person of the only begotten Son of God, the Lord Jesus Christ. Here are three of the many Bible passages that teach this marvelous truth.

- "In the beginning was the Word, and the Word was with God, and the Word was God...And the Word was made flesh, and dwelt among us, (and we beheld his glory, the glory as of the only begotten of the Father,) full of grace and truth" (John 1:1,14).

- "Jesus saith unto him, Have I been so long time with you, and yet hast thou not known me, Philip? He that hath seen me hath seen the Father" (John 14:9).

- "For in [Christ] dwelleth all the fulness of the Godhead bodily" (Colossians 2:9).

Just as space is made visible and understandable by matter, so God the Son, the Messiah, Jesus of Nazareth, makes God the Father visible and understandable by His presence on earth. And just as space and matter are one in the sense that they are inseparable and coterminous at all times, so God the Father and God the Son are one (John 10:30). And just as time is the vital element through which mankind can experience everything that can be known in his small part of the universe, so God the Holy Spirit is the person of the triune Godhead through whom man is enabled to experience both the Father and the Son. Again, many Bible passages tell of the Holy Spirit's role in salvation, spiritual guidance, and growing awareness of the person and work of Christ. Here are a few of the more obvious texts.

- "If I go not away, the Comforter will not come unto you... And when he is come, he will reprove the world of sin, and of righteousness, and of judgment" (John 16:7-8).

- "God hath from the beginning chosen you to salvation through sanctification of the Spirit and belief of the truth" (2 Thessalonians 2:13).

- "That which is born of the Spirit is spirit. Marvel not that

I said unto thee, Ye must be born again…So is every one that is born of the Spirit" (John 3:6-8).

- "Howbeit when he, the Spirit of truth, is come, he will guide you into all truth" (John 16:13).

The Godhead is the triune Deity who created the universe (Romans 1:20; Colossians 2:9). That universe is the only accurate picture of His divine nature (2 Peter 1:4), having been created by God to provide a totally accessible foundation by which one can know that the Creator exists (Romans 1:19-21). That universally available knowledge enables mankind to "believe that he is, and that he is a rewarder of them that diligently seek him" (Hebrews 11:6).

The one ongoing act of creation that God continues to perform is the new birth of those who are "created in righteousness and true holiness" (Ephesians 4:24). Men and women are born into this world spiritually "dead in trespasses and sins" (Ephesians 2:1) and must pass "from death unto life" (John 5:24). That change produces a new man (Colossians 3:10) that is "made free from sin" (Romans 6:18) so that everyone can be "partakers of the divine nature" (2 Peter 1:4), where "old things are passed away" and "all things are become new" (2 Corinthians 5:17).

God's Holiness

God's preeminent attribute is holiness. This unique nature both drives and limits God's revelation of Himself to His creation. "There is none holy as the LORD: for there is none beside thee" (1 Samuel 2:2; see also Exodus 15:11; Isaiah 6:3).

This holiness requires truth. God cannot lie (Titus 1:2), and whenever God reveals anything, He must reveal the truth about Himself and His nature.

> Wherein God, willing more abundantly to show unto the heirs of promise the immutability of his counsel, confirmed it by an oath: that by two immutable things, in which it was impossible for God to lie, we might have a strong consolation (Hebrews 6:17-18).

That biblical axiom is true whether applied to scientific research, educational philosophy, theological speculations, or heretical doctrine. "What if some did not believe? Shall their unbelief make the faith of God without effect? God forbid: yea, let God be true, but every man a liar" (Romans 3:3-4; see also John 14:6; 1 John 5:20).

The incarnate Creator God must reveal truth. When God speaks, He must speak the truth; when God acts, He must do the truth.

> These things saith he that is holy, he that is true, he that hath the key of David, he that openeth, and no man shutteth; and shutteth, and no man openeth…These things saith the Amen, the faithful and true witness, the beginning of the creation of God (Revelation 3:7,14; see also John 8:31-32; 2 Corinthians 1:18-20).

God's holiness demands that the creation not distort anything about Him or about the creation itself. God could not create a lie. He could not make anything that would inexorably lead to a wrong conclusion. God could not create processes that would counter His own nature or that would lead man to conclude something untrue about God.

> God could not create processes that would counter His own nature.

Because of these sacred truths, the agelong processes required by evolutionary naturalism are absolutely incompatible with the demands of a holy Creator. The words of the biblical text do not use the same order, employ the same language, or imply the same concepts. God is truly holy, so a very difficult and complex deconstruction and interpretation of the text is necessary to allow for a combination or hybridization of these two very different ideas. God's holiness required Him to create a perfect garden, for instance, fully formed and beautiful at the moment of its first creation.

It is because of man—once perfect, created last—that the world fell to ruin.

God's Omniscience

Today, the most easily observable attribute of God is His omniscience. The unlimited power of God (His omnipotence) is displayed in the apparently infinite universe containing the immeasurable energy resources in the uncounted galaxies of space. Certainly they speak of God's eternal power. But in the last few decades, humanity has become more aware of the infinitely complex nature of this universe. From the vast majesty of the stellar host to the minute beauty of microscopic living organisms, the incredible design and order of the world is becoming more and more evident.

The universe is an infinite reservoir of information.

Within the past decade, the vast information of the genome has stunned scientists. It includes instructions for biological development of the specific life form as well as languages within languages, repair codes, timing signals, duplication mechanisms...an entire library of information that is unique for each of the millions of reproducing living systems on earth. The old academic cliché "The more I know, the more I know I don't know" has never been more true than it is today.

There is no such thing as a simple cell. If it is alive, it is most definitely not simple.

So where did all this information come from? Certainly not from inanimate matter. Chemicals and amino acids and proteins are not information-generating systems. They may be like letters in the words used in instructions, but they do not produce the information. There is order and functioning precision at every level of the universe. How did such order and precision get there? Certainly not from an explosion and a random drift of interacting molecules. Randomness (chaos) never produces order and precision. The information so readily and easily observable in the universe fairly screams for a Designer.

The only reason people do not believe in an omniscient Creator is that they refuse to believe.

The Bible emphasizes God's omniscience.

Throughout the text of God's Word, we find many sections that tell about the infinite mind of the Creator. His purposes and means are perfect and guided by wisdom and design, not drifting randomly in evolutionary confusion. God's decisions do not change or falter, but are the assured perfection of holy goodness and absolute knowledge. Everything from the beginning of time has been determined "according to the good pleasure of his will" (Ephesians 1:5). Here are a few of the many Scriptures that speak of God's omniscience.

- "I am God, and there is none else; I am God, and there is none like me, declaring the end from the beginning, and from ancient times the things that are not yet done, saying, My counsel shall stand, and I will do all my pleasure" (Isaiah 46:9-10).

- "Known unto God are all his works from the beginning of the world" (Acts 15:18).

- "…to the acknowledgement of the mystery of God, and of the Father, and of Christ; in whom are hid all the treasures of wisdom and knowledge" (Colossians 2:2-3).

Human language is not sufficient to perfectly convey the entire concept of omniscience, but here are several key elements:

- God is aware of everything.

- God cannot be progressively aware.

- God's knowledge is immediate.

- God is free from imperfection.

- God knows all there is to know.

God keeps some secrets.

Some things in God's plan for the universe in general and for man in particular are kept secret until the planned events become a reality. Some reasons and processes are far too complex for fallen man to comprehend. Much of the future would be terrifying to contemplate if the details were known in advance. It is far better for us to trust the all-knowing, loving, and patient Creator to reveal what we need to know. "The secret things belong unto the LORD our God: but those things which are revealed belong unto us and to our children for ever" (Deuteronomy 29:29; see also 1 Corinthians 13:12; 2 Peter 1:3).

God, the omniscient One, must reveal complete information—or He must withhold information (the "secret things"). Any partial revelation, when presented as though it is all of the information, would be a lie. *Half-truth* is nothing but a sanitized term for a lie. God cannot lie, and therefore He cannot say or do anything that would be either partially true or imperfectly functioning. God can and sometimes does make statements that reveal large truths without giving specific details, such as "My kingdom is not of this world" (John 18:36). But God would never speak or do anything that would mislead man.

God is never random or confused.

There is no hint of randomness in God. God is never surprised so that He must react to unforeseen circumstances. Neither is God forced to change His mind about His reasons or His plans. He does not alter His plans for eternity, nor does He get confused about His design, His pleasure, or His purpose. "Whatsoever the LORD pleased, that did he in heaven, and in earth, in the seas, and all deep places" (Psalm 135:6). God's purposes are ordered and flow from His omniscience. His decisions are unchangeable and without confusion. His specific will and pleasure are always implemented. "My counsel shall stand, and I will do all my pleasure…I have spoken it, I will also bring it to pass; I have purposed it, I will also do it" (Isaiah 46:10-11; see also Psalm 33:11; 1 Corinthians 14:33; Ephesians 1:9-11; Hebrews 6:17-19).

God's omniscience demands that He create only the absolute best, whether at the scale of the universe or the scale of the molecule. He could not and would not experiment or produce an inferior product. Because God knows what is best, He therefore must do that best. He must create, shape, and make only that which is good. It is no accident or verbal hyperbole that the text of Genesis 1 repeats, "and God saw that it was good." Neither is it merely for poetic parallelism that at the end of the sixth and final day of God's creating work, the text reads, "And God saw everything that he had made, and, behold, it was very good" (Genesis 1:31).

> God's omniscience demands that He create only the absolute best, whether at the scale of the universe or the scale of the molecule.

So-called theistic evolution (like the various other Christian attempts to hybridize the words of Scripture and the theories of naturalistic evolution) requires both experimentation with creation and the creation of inferior forms. In evolution, there is no permanent good. Evolutionary naturalism requires processes and activities that are contradictory to God's nature.

The early 1990s witnessed a revival of theistic evolution, which received a good bit of favorable press through the Evangelical Theological Society and the American Scientific Affiliation—organizations that insisted that they support biblical inspiration but see no difficulties in accepting evolutionary mechanisms as God's method of creation. Remember the statement by Professor David Hull about the incompatibility of biblical creation and evolution?

> The evolutionary process is rife with happenstance, contingency, incredible waste, death, pain and horror...[Theistic evolution's God] is not a loving God who cares about His productions. [He] is careless, wasteful, indifferent, almost diabolical. He is certainly not the sort of God to whom anyone would be inclined to pray.[1]

Apparently, godless scholars are more aware of the impossibility of mixing the two belief systems than are those Christians who insist that there is no problem. Significant time has elapsed since Dr. Hull wrote his critique of theistic evolution, but the acceptance of the hybrid theories has been eclipsed only by the apathy of Christians who see no importance in the doctrine of creation.

Summarizing the Evidence

The triunity of creation. Space, matter, and time are the components of the creation itself and analogous to the Father, Son, and Holy Spirit.

The attributes of God. Evolutionary ideas run counter to holiness—God's preeminent attribute.

The infinite mind of the Creator. God's omniscience will not allow Him to create or act in randomness.

Biblical Insight

Read the accounts of creation and the fall in Genesis 1–3.

1. What purposeful actions does God demonstrate?

2. Does anything in these verses suggest God's ignorance?

3. How does God demonstrate His holiness in chapter 3?

13

God's Purpose for Creation Precludes Evolution

 God expressed His will through His act of creating, as these verses clearly show.

- "Thou art worthy, O Lord, to receive glory and honor and power: for thou hast created all things, and for thy pleasure they are and were created" (Revelation 4:11).

- "By him were all things created, that are in heaven, and that are in earth, visible and invisible...all things were created by him, and for him: and he is before all things, and by him all things consist" (Colossians 1:16-17).

- "Of him, and through him, and to him, are all things: to whom be glory for ever. Amen" (Romans 11:36).

Once again, when we see what the Scriptures reveal about the nature of God and about His purpose of creating the universe—to please God and to honor God—we realize that He could not possibly have used any form of naturalistic evolution to create that which would forever speak of His person and work. If the words of Scripture are true words, if they are God's words, there can be no evolution in God's work.

> If the words of Scripture are true words, if they are God's words, there can be no evolution in God's work.

God's act of creation eliminates excuses to deny His existence.

For some reason, many Christians seem to think that God is somehow unfair to nations and people who haven't heard the gospel. Subtle doubts about God showing favoritism or about His salvation methods being arbitrary creep into these people's personal theology. As a result, they try desperately to devise ways in which God gives a second chance or has a more tolerant judgment for those who don't have an opportunity to accept Jesus as their personal Savior. But as we have seen, God has revealed Himself to everyone.

- "The invisible things of him from the creation of the world are clearly seen, being understood by the things that are made, even his eternal power and Godhead; so that they are without excuse" (Romans 1:20).

- "The heavens declare the glory of God; and the firmament showeth his handiwork. Day unto day uttereth speech, and night unto night showeth knowledge. There is no speech nor language, where their voice is not heard" (Psalm 19:1-3).

The Bible is clear. God has done everything necessary for all men to know that He exists. He draws all men to Christ (John 12:32). He reveals Himself to all who seek Him with all their heart (Jeremiah 29:13). Conversely, God rejects all those who change "the glory of the uncorruptible God into an image made like to corruptible man, and to birds, and fourfooted beasts, and creeping things" (Romans 1:23). These people have changed "the truth of God into a lie, and worshipped and served the creature more than the Creator" (verse 25). Consequently, "God gave them over to a reprobate mind" (verse 28).

God's act of creation provides a foundation for the everlasting gospel.

The gospel of Jesus Christ entails the full threefold work of Christ: He is the Creator, He is the One who presently conserves all things, and He will finally consummate all things unto Himself (Colossians 1:16-17). If the creation message is neglected, there is no foundation for or evidence of God's omnipotent ability to save. If the work of Christ on the cross of Calvary is neglected, there is no reconciliation of God's holiness toward sinners. And if the promise of a sinless, completely righteous, deathless future in a new heaven and new earth is neglected, there is no hope. The everlasting gospel sits solidly on the foundation of the creation reality.

> And I saw another angel fly in the midst of heaven, having the everlasting gospel to preach unto them that dwell on the earth…saying with a loud voice, Fear God, and give glory to him; for the hour of his judgment is come: and worship him that made heaven, and earth, and the sea, and the fountains of waters (Revelation 14:6-7).

God's act of creation provides authority to the message of Jesus Christ.

Jesus once said to His struggling disciples, "The words that I speak unto you I speak not of myself: but the Father that dwelleth in me, he doeth the works. Believe me that I am in the Father, and the Father in me: or else believe me for the very works' sake" (John 14:10-11). He said essentially the same thing to the unbelieving religious leaders: "Then came the Jews round about him, and said unto him, How long dost thou make us to doubt? If thou be the Christ, tell us plainly. Jesus answered them, I told you, and ye believed not: the works that I do in my Father's name, they bear witness of me" (John 10:24-25).

John's Gospel is built around seven great miracles of creation. These were miracles that required the creation of new matter (water turned into wine); new functioning organs (blind eyes made well); and new bone, muscles, and nerves (a withered arm restored). Again and again, Jesus demonstrated His creation power before the masses. Although "the common people heard him gladly" (Mark 12:37), the religious leaders plotted to kill Him.

> By him were all things created, that are in heaven, and that are in earth, visible and invisible…all things were created by him, and for him: and he is before all things, and by him all things consist. And he is the head of the body, the

church: who is the beginning, the firstborn from the dead; that in all things he might have the preeminence (Colossians 1:16-18).

God's act of creation displayed the power of Jesus Christ.

This is similar to the authority issue. The prologue to John's Gospel emphasizes that the Word was God from eternity past and equal in every respect as the Son of God within the Trinity, yet He was made flesh and entered the world that He had created in order to redeem those whom He had created.

> In the beginning was the Word, and the Word was with God, and the Word was God. The same was in the beginning with God. All things were made by him; and without him was not any thing made that was made. In him was life; and the life was the light of men…But as many as received him, to them gave he power to become the sons of God, even to them that believe on his name… And the Word was made flesh, and dwelt among us, (and we beheld his glory, the glory as of the only begotten of the Father,) full of grace and truth (John 1:1-4,12,14).

The truth about creation gives the substitutionary work of Jesus Christ both its legitimacy as the fully human substitute for humanity and its infinite power as the full Deity and Creator satisfied the judgment of a Holy God for the "sins of the whole world" (1 John 2:2).

God gives new life through the act of creation.

Even though God rested from His creation of the space-matter-time universe on the seventh day, He continues creating the new man as men and women and children of all ages come to Him as Redeemer and Savior.

> By grace are ye saved through faith; and that not of yourselves: it is the gift of God: not of works, lest any man should boast. For we are his workmanship, created in

Christ Jesus unto good works, which God hath before ordained that we should walk in them (Ephesians 2:8-10).

For this, as well as for all the other great works of the Lord Jesus Christ, mankind should be forever grateful. You and I should be grateful. He is now sitting in the throne room of heaven, mediating and serving as High Priest and Advocate for us. Therefore, we should constantly praise Him. He is the One who will one day (perhaps soon) reign as King of kings and Lord of lords, so we should expectantly pray for His kingdom to come and for His will to be done in earth, as it is in heaven (Matthew 6:10).

Even so, Lord Jesus, come quickly.

Summarizing the Evidence

God's purpose. The creation of this world and life demonstrate that God acts with purpose.

God's plan. Even in the face of rebellion, God's plan of redemption for those He created could not be thwarted.

New creatures. Each time a sinner comes to Christ, a new creation is born according to the Creator's plan.

Biblical Insight

Study Ephesians 2:8-10.

1. New life results from whose initiative?

2. What can man do to be recreated in Christ?

3. How long has God desired to redeem and recreate mankind?

14

Why Is Biblical Creationism Important?

Biblical creationism is foundational to all Christian doctrine.
Christ was Creator before He became Redeemer (John 1:3; Colossians 1:16; Hebrews 1:2-3). Unless, therefore, the presentation of the person and work of Christ is based on His role as Creator, what is being taught is actually "another Jesus." Paul strongly warns against such false teaching and perversions of the gospel of Christ in 2 Corinthians 11:4 and Galatians 1:7-8.

The first object of a living faith and a saving faith (Hebrews 10:38-39) is a solid belief in special creation: "Through faith we understand that the worlds were framed by the word of God, so that things which are seen were not made of things which do appear" (Hebrews 11:3). This negates theistic evolution, which assumes that everything in the present was created from other things in the past. It therefore demands a meaningful faith built on special creation.

Biblical creationism is the foundation of true evangelism.
John's Gospel is built on its opening words: "In the beginning was the Word." This echoes the first book of the Bible and ties it to the importance of knowing the creating work of Christ. When Christians confess that "Jesus is the Christ, the Son of God" so that they "might have life through his name," they are confessing their belief in every aspect of Christ's nature and role, including His role as Creator (John 20:31).

True missions work begins with biblical creationism.

When the polytheistic evolutionists of Lystra were given the gospel, they were reprimanded with the following words: "Ye should turn from these vanities unto the living God, which made heaven, and earth, and the sea, and all things that are therein" (Acts 14:15). And to the atheistic evolutionist Epicureans and the pantheistic evolutionist Stoics in Athens, Paul said, "God that made the world and all things therein…is Lord of heaven and earth" (Acts 17:24). When Paul delivered the gospel to people who already believed in the Scriptures, including creation, he always began at Jesus and gave the gospel of the cross and resurrection. But to those who did not believe, he began with the creation truth.

Biblical creationism is the foundation of true Bible teaching.

When Christ spoke on the road to Emmaus, "beginning at Moses and all the prophets, he expounded unto them in all the scriptures the things concerning himself" (Luke 24:27). Christ revealed Himself to His walking companions beginning with the first things: His creative work recorded in the words of Moses.

Paul's goal in his preaching to the churches was to show them the true "fellowship of the mystery, which from the beginning of the world hath been hid in God, who created all things by Jesus Christ: to the intent that now unto the principalities and powers in heavenly places might be known by the church the manifold wisdom of God" (Ephesians 3:9-10). God's creating work gives the church a common theme in its worship and a fellowship as children of their Creator.

Recognizing God as Creator and head of the church is the start of a hierarchy that He models. Christ details that hierarchy with concern to the household and family relationships in Matthew.

> He answered and said unto them, Have ye not read, that he which made them at the beginning made them male and female, and said, For this cause shall a man leave father and mother, and shall cleave to his wife: and they twain shall be one flesh? Wherefore they are no more twain, but one flesh. What therefore God hath joined together, let not man put asunder (Matthew 19:4-6).

Christ is the head of the church, the firstborn of all creation, just as man is head over his wife, having been created before her.

Biblical creationism provides a model for all human vocations.

In Genesis 1:28, God gave the dominion mandate: "Be fruitful, and multiply, and replenish the earth, and subdue it: and have dominion over the fish of the sea, and over the fowl of the air, and over every living thing that moveth upon the earth." This primeval command encompasses all honorable human occupations.

science to understand the earth

technology to develop it

commerce to utilize it

education to transmit the knowledge of it

humanities to glorify it

Every occupation may be used in some way to glorify God and recognize man's responsibility to God's creation by obeying this first command of dominion over the earth. Beyond occupational services to God's creation, man has his own specific purpose. The image of God in man has been marred by sin, but when he is created again by the new birth, he can begin to live the kind of life for which God created man in the beginning. The new creature may be daily renewed to be more like his Father and closer to the holiness that he was intended to know (2 Corinthians 5:17; Ephesians 4:24).

Once a biblical worldview has been adopted, including a proper understanding of creation and redemption, the Christian believer will rightly relate to other Christians, society around him, and the Creator-Redeemer Himself, who has reconciled all things to God. In order for the true gospel to be preached, the full scope of God's work must be told, for it is only the true gospel, wholly and uncompromising, that is the power of God unto salvation (Romans 1:16). This gospel encompasses the threefold work of Christ: creation, conservation, and consummation. If the gospel story neglects the creation of the past, there is no foundation, standard, or ability. If it neglects the cross, there is no authority, justness, or power. And if it neglects the coming kingdom, there is no hope or joy or victory.

The church has been working hard and effectually on the central aspect of the gospel, but it is time to reaffirm its commitment to preach the whole counsel of God (Acts 20:27) and teach the foundation and consummation of God's wondrous work as well.[1]

15

Genesis and the Gospel

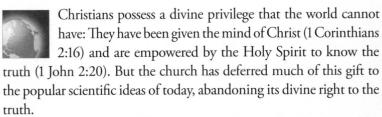Christians possess a divine privilege that the world cannot have: They have been given the mind of Christ (1 Corinthians 2:16) and are empowered by the Holy Spirit to know the truth (1 John 2:20). But the church has deferred much of this gift to the popular scientific ideas of today, abandoning its divine right to the truth.

It has become popular to believe that winning souls is more important than adhering to the clear biblical truth—that if certain biblical doctrines conflict with the conclusions of secular science, they can be ignored or cast aside in order to "by all means save some" (1 Corinthians 9:22). However, this is the very reason why so many churches are still doctrinally and morally weak. Many people are thirsting for something stronger than ambiguous stories and unanswered questions on the origins of life, and they seek confirmation of the holy nature of a God who is often portrayed as cruel and untrustworthy.

How can the church impact the world for Christ if so many professing Christians mistrust their God and the revelation He gave to them? Why accommodate the secular and often blatantly atheistic world when the biblical worldview answers the many questions that the world cannot? The Bible offers the power of the true gospel, and despite the protestations of a relativistic culture, people are hungry for the truth.

The Central Gospel Message

Almost every person who has gone to a Christian church knows that Christ commanded His disciples to reach the whole world with the proclamation of the gospel message. The New Testament Greek word most often translated *gospel* is *euaggelion*. The verb form is *euaggelizo*, from which our English word *evangelize* is derived. The basic meaning of those two Greek words is simply "good message." The English word *gospel* is shortened from the Saxon phrase *God's spell*, meaning God's news.

It is interesting to note that *gospel* appears precisely 101 times in the New Testament. Centrally positioned right in the middle of these references—fifty before and fifty after—is 1 Corinthians 15:1-4.

> I declare unto you the gospel which I preached unto you, which also ye have received, and wherein ye stand; by which also ye are saved, if ye keep in memory what I preached unto you, unless ye have believed in vain. For I delivered unto you first of all that which I also received, how that Christ died for our sins according to the scriptures; and that he was buried, and that he rose again the third day according to the scriptures.

This is the defining biblical passage for the gospel. The focus is the death, physical burial, and bodily resurrection of Christ. This message is to be received and believed by faith, once and for all. It is the means by which men are saved, continually and forever. These are the facts—the unyielding truth—upon which men may firmly stand. They are emphatically defined by, understood by means of, and declared according to the Scriptures. The gospel is not to be adapted to fit the context of one's environment or personal preference. It is to be proclaimed singularly, precisely, and persistently as an absolute truth that God has revealed.

Apart from the work of Jesus Christ on the cross, there is no forgiveness.

The Hope of the Gospel

Most certainly the forgiveness of our sins is good news. Our sins are cast behind God's back (Isaiah 38:17). They have been removed from us "as far as the east is from the west" (Psalm 103:12), and from the human perspective, those sins have been cast "into the depths of the sea" (Micah 7:19). But as marvelously wonderful as that knowledge may be, there is more!

The first biblical reference to the gospel is recorded in Matthew 4:23. Christ came "preaching the gospel of the kingdom." In the very beginning of His ministry, Jesus announced (preached) the good news that He was there to fulfill (to consummate) the promises made to the patriarchs for those who were or would become His people. One day, all creation will acknowledge Jesus Christ as the "Lord of lords, and King of kings" (Revelation 17:14). For those who have received His grace-gift of salvation (John 1:12), this will bring joy "unspeakable and full of glory" (1 Peter 1:8) before the great throne in the courts of heaven. For those who have rejected His love and spurned the witness of the Holy Spirit, the awful realization of their eternal damnation will come in a whirlwind of fear and destruction (Proverbs 1:27).

The good news of the message of the gospel is summarized in the last two chapters of Revelation. The New Jerusalem, the capital city of King Jesus, is described in these glorious passages, and God gives a formal declaration to the redeemed.

> I heard a great voice out of heaven saying, Behold, the tabernacle of God is with men, and he will dwell with them, and they shall be his people, and God himself shall be with them, and be their God. And God shall wipe away all tears from their eyes; and there shall be no more death, neither sorrow, nor crying, neither shall there be any more pain: for the former things are passed away (Revelation 21:3-4).

An absolutely vital part of the gospel is the stunning news that our salvation will consummate in a permanent and eternal "new heavens and a new earth, wherein dwelleth righteousness" (2 Peter 3:13). This future hope of a righteous life for eternity with the Creator-God sustained the Lord Jesus as He faced a horrible and ignominious death by crucifixion: "...who for the joy that was set before him endured the cross, despising the shame" (Hebrews 12:2). Paul the apostle commented, "If in this life only we have hope in Christ, we are of all men most miserable" (1 Corinthians 15:19).

Apart from the promise of a future eternal righteous life, there is no hope.

The Authority for the Gospel Message

And yet there is more. Indeed, there must be more! Where does the authority to grant forgiveness come from? Where does the power to rebuild a universe in perfection come from? How can sinful men be made sinless? Where? How? What can we see that will assure us that the promises of forgiveness and an eternal destiny of righteousness will be real?

Yes, Jesus Christ rose from the grave, having conquered death, and gave "assurance unto all men" (Acts 17:31). That too is part of the gospel (Romans 10:9). But where did that power come from? How can we find faith in that which is so supernatural that our natural minds see only foolishness (1 Corinthians 2:14)?

God did not leave the answers to that problem out of His good news. Part and parcel of the gospel is the unshakable foundation and omnipotent display of the creation of the universe.

The very last verse in the Bible to cite the gospel extends the scope of the good message to the everlasting gospel. This section in Revelation 14 tells of a mighty angel who is commissioned to fly throughout the entire atmosphere of the earth...

> ...having the everlasting gospel to preach unto them that dwell on the earth, and to every nation, and kindred, and tongue, and people, saying with a loud voice, Fear God, and give glory to him; for the hour of his judgment is come: and worship him that made heaven, and earth, and the sea, and the fountains of waters (Revelation 14:6-7).

Here the emphasis is on the creation—the origin of the good message. Jesus, the One who hung on the cross of Calvary as the full substitute for the sins of the whole world, is also the One who created the whole world. The One who cried out in the most incomprehensible statement of grace and mercy ever uttered, "Father, forgive them; for they know not what they do" (Luke 23:34), is the same One who simply commanded: "Let there be light: and there was light" (Genesis 1:3).

For by him were all things created, that are in heaven, and that are in earth, visible and invisible, whether they be thrones, or dominions, or principalities, or powers: all things were created by him, and for him: And he is before all things, and by him all things consist. And he is the head of the body, the church: who is the beginning, the firstborn from the dead; that in all things he might have the preeminence. For it pleased the Father that in him should all fullness dwell; And, having made peace through the blood of his cross, by him to reconcile all things unto himself; by him, I say, whether they be things in earth, or things in heaven (Colossians 1:16-20).

The Full Gospel

The gospel message entails the full scope of the work of Jesus Christ, involving the whole sweep of His redemptive purpose in history. Everything from the beginning of creation to the triumphal day when every living creature, at last, will confess the truth of Christ's lordship (Philippians 2:11) is part of God's great redemptive plan. The gospel does not finish with a mere salvation from death, just as it does not begin with Christ's death on the cross. It begins with His work of creation.

It is Christ who first created the heavens and earth, and having created them, ended His creative work (Colossians 1:16). All things continue to exist, conserved as mass and energy (verse 17), but it is by His will alone, for His purposes, and for His sake that creation continues its existence. Finally, these verses speak of the beautiful reconciliation made by Christ's death, not only with man, but with the creation itself (verse 20). Through Christ's blood, earth and heaven may be restored to harmony. No longer an enemy of God, this once alienated world may be brought again into a universal concord, conformed to the government of its Creator.

Hebrews 1:2-3 reiterates that God, through Christ, created the worlds, and that Christ will be the heir of all things—the nations and the earth—as reigning Lord (Psalm 2:8), "for of him, and through him, and to him, are all things: to whom be glory for ever. Amen" (Romans 11:36). The gospel of the Lord Jesus Christ encompasses a threefold work: creation, conservation, and consummation. Christ was present before time began, He continues His work of upholding His creation, and one day He will be finally recognized as King and Lord of all.

In the past, present, and future, God's love and glory are evident in His great work of creation, and every part of His plan must be addressed in the gospel if it is to be proclaimed with confidence in its everlasting truth. If the act of creation is neglected in the presentation of the gospel, then the very foundation of God's plan is lost and the authority He has over life and all things is forgotten. If the cross is neglected, then Christ has no authority over death and no power of salvation or reconciliation to God. To neglect the kingdom is to abandon any hope or present joy.

However, to embrace the full gospel means to take hold of all that Christ our Creator has promised for us. We can live with confidence that we were indeed made "very good" by Him, unique from all other creatures, fit for good works, from before the foundation of the world.

We can live with assurance that we have been forgiven and cleansed from the sin that has plagued mankind since Adam, kneeling with gratitude in His presence because of the sacrificial atonement of Jesus Christ.

And we can live with real hope and deep joy knowing that Christ, our Creator and Savior, will fulfill every one of His promises to restore us fully to the Father and make us able to stand faultless before the throne of heaven.

> And I heard a great voice out of heaven saying, Behold, the tabernacle of God is with men, and he will dwell with them, and they shall be his people, and God himself shall be with them, and be their God. And God shall wipe away all tears from their eyes; there shall be no more death, nor sorrow, nor crying, neither shall there be any more pain: for the former things are passed away. And he that sat upon the throne said, Behold, I make all things new (Revelation 21:3-5).

Notes

Chapter 1: Evidence for God

Epigraph. Barry Parker, *Creation: The Story of the Origin and Evolution of the Universe* (New York: Basic Books, 2003), 282.

1. "Open Theism Information." www.opentheism.info, accessed November 30, 2009.

2. David L. Hull, "The God of the Galápagos" *Nature*, vol. 352, no. 6335 (1991), 486.

3. C.S. Lewis, *Mere Christianity* (New York: Macmillan, 1952), 30.

4. Peter Kreeft, *The Argument from Conscience.* Available online at www.peterkreeft.com/topics/conscience.htm.

5. Dallas Willard, *The Divine Conspiracy: Rediscovering Our Hidden Life in God* (San Francisco: HarperSanFrancisco, 1998), 317.

6. Francis Schaeffer, *A Christian Manifesto* (Westchester, IL: Crossway Books, 1981), 17-18.

Chapter 2: Evidence for Truth

1. Norman L. Geisler and Ronald M. Brooks, *Come Let Us Reason: An Introduction to Logical Thinking* (Grand Rapids, MI: Baker Books, 1990), 16.

2. Eugene Wigner, "The Unreasonable Effectiveness of Mathematics in the Natural Sciences," *Communications in Pure and Applied Mathematics,* vol. 13, no. 1 (1960).

3. Albert Einstein, *Sidelights on Relativity* (New York: Dover, 1983).

4. John Bunyan, *The Holy War* (New Kensington, PA: Whitaker House, 2001), 31.

Chapter 3: Evidence from Nature

Epigraph. Paul Davies, *The Cosmic Blueprint: New Discoveries in Nature's Creative Ability to Order the Universe* (New York: Simon and Schuster, 1988), 203.

1. "If you use the word catastrophic it rubs some people the wrong way, but something dramatic happened on Venus which wiped out almost all signs of an older surface." (Planetary scientist David Grinspoon, quoted in Henry Bortman, "Venus: Hothouse Planet," *Astrobiology Magazine,* www.astrobio.net/interview/1137/venus-hothouse-planet.)

2. Danny Faulkner, "Blue Stars—Unexpected Brilliance," *Answers*, vol. 6, no. 1 (2010), 50-53.

3. Faulkner, "Blue Stars," 50-53.

4. Cheryl. Gundy, "NASA's Hubble Finds Rare 'Blue Straggler' Stars in Milky Way's Hub," NASA news release, May 25, 2011.

Chapter 4: Evidence from Physical Science

1. Carey M. Lisse, et al., "Spitzer Space Telescope Observations of the Nucleus of Comet 103P/Hartley 2," *Publications of the Astronomical Society of the Pacific*, vol. 121, no. 883 (2009), 968-75.

Chapter 5: Evidence from Earth Science

1. Andrew A. Snelling, "Radiocarbon Ages for Fossil Ammonites and Wood in Cretaceous Strata near Redding, California," *Answers Research Journal*, vol. 1 (2008), 123-44.

2. Johan Lindgren, et al., "Microspectroscopic Evidence of Cretaceous Bone Proteins," *PLoS ONE*, vol. 6, no. 4 (2011), e19, 445.

Chapter 6: Evidence from Life Science

1. Carl Holm, "Life Elements Came from Space," March 1, 2011. news.discovery.com/space/life-elements-space-110301.html.

2. Richard Dawkins, "Evolution: The next 200 years," *New Scientist*, no. 2693 (2009), 41.

3. Ann Gibbons, "Mitochondrial Eve refuses to die," *Science*, vol. 259, no. 5099 (1993), 1249-50. See also Ann Gibbons, "Calibrating the Mitochondrial Clock," *Science*, vol. 279, no. 5347 (1998), 28-29; R. Carter, "Mitochondrial diversity within modern human populations," *Nucleic Acids Research*, vol. 35, no. 9 (2007), 3039-45.

4. R.L. Dorit, H. Akashi, and W. Gilbert, "Absence of polymorphism at the *ZFY* locus on the human Y chromosome," *Science*, vol. 268 (1995), 1183-85.

5. John Morris and Frank Sherwin showed the fundamental disagreements among evolutionists over the status of a hundred or so supposedly transitional forms in their book *The Fossil Record* (Dallas: Institute for Creation Research, 2010). Their chief secular sources were E.H. Colbert, M. Morales, and E.C. Minkoff, *Colbert's Evolution of the Vertebrates*, 5th ed. (New York: Wiley-Liss, 2001); and M.J. Benton, *Vertebrate Paleontology* (Malden, MA: Blackwell Science, 2005).

6. J. Baumgardner, J. Sanford, W. Brewer, P. Gibson, and W. ReMine, "Mendel's Accountant: A biologically realistic forward-time population genetics program" *Scalable Computing Practice and Experience*, vol. 8, no. 2 (2007), 147-65.

Chapter 7: Evidence from Scripture

1. International Council on Biblical Inerrancy, "Chicago Statement on Biblical Inerrancy" (1978).

Chapter 11: There Is No Evidence Evolution Took Place in the Past

1. Henry M. Morris, "The Profusion of Living Fossils," *Acts & Facts*, vol. 29, no. 11 (2000).

2. R.C. Lewontin, "Billions and Billions of Demons: Review of *The Demon-Haunted World: Science as a Candle in the Dark* by Carl Sagan," *The New York Review of Books*, vol. 44, no. 1 (1997), 31.

Chapter 12: God's Character Precludes Evolutionary Methods

1. David L. Hull, "The God of the Galápagos," *Nature*, vol. 352, no. 6335 (1991), 486.

Chapter 14: Why Is Biblical Creationism Important?

2. Adapted from H.M. Morris, *Biblical Creationism* (Green Forest, AR: Master Books, 2000), 228-32.

About the Author

Henry M. Morris III serves as chief executive officer of the Institute for Creation Research in Dallas, Texas. He holds four earned degrees, including a D.Min. from Luther Rice Seminary and the Presidents and Key Executives MBA from Pepperdine University. A former college professor, administrator, business executive, and senior pastor, Dr. Morris is an articulate and passionate speaker who is frequently invited to address church congregations, college assemblies, and national conferences.

The eldest son of the founder of ICR, Dr. Morris has served for many years in conference and writing ministry. His love for the Word of God and passion for Christian maturity, coupled with God's gift of teaching, has given Dr. Morris a broad and effective ministry over the years. He has also written numerous articles and several books.

To learn more about Harvest House books and
to read sample chapters, log on to our website:

www.harvesthousepublishers.com

HARVEST HOUSE PUBLISHERS
EUGENE, OREGON